*Twayne's English Authors Series*

Sylvia E. Bowman, *Editor*

INDIANA UNIVERSITY

*Thomas Middleton*

TEAS 139

# Thomas Middleton

By NORMAN A. BRITTIN

*Auburn University*

Twayne Publishers, Inc. :: New York

Library of Congress Catalog Card Number: 76-187617



MANUFACTURED IN THE UNITED STATES OF AMERICA

# *Preface*

In 1938 Joseph Quincy Adams complained in his Foreword to R. C. Bald's edition of *Hengist, King of Kent* that Thomas Middleton was the most neglected of major dramatists of his period, and he called for much more scholarly work on Middleton's biography, on the canon and chronology of his plays, and on their textual problems. Since his call to labor, much has been achieved; for, building on the accomplishments of Mildred Christian, W. D. Dunkel, and R. C. Bald, a considerable number of scholars have greatly advanced our knowledge of Middleton. Tribute must be paid especially to Mark Eccles, R. H. Barker, George R. Price, Samuel Schoenbaum, Richard Levin, and the editors of certain Middleton plays recently issued. Many others made contributions in all the areas that Adams mentioned. While much remains to be done, it is no longer true that scholarship or criticism is neglecting Middleton.

The aim of this book is to provide a guide to the whole body of Middleton's work in the light of contemporary scholarship. Historians of the drama see Middleton not only as a representative figure in the Jacobean age, which is the greatest period of English drama, but also as the most important writer in that era of the comedy of manners. One might say that he stands midway between Ben Jonson and John Fletcher: he shares with Jonson something of the satirical, moralizing impulse; and he imparts to Fletcher a satirical observation, pervaded with a gay, farcical spirit, of city life. In addition, Middleton's tragedies are imbued with exceptional realism and power.

In accordance with prevailing critical views of the mid-twentieth century, this study emphasizes Middleton's powers of construction, his psychological penetration, his realistic social settings, the appropriateness of his style at its best, and his almost-modern intelligence. On the basis of these qualities, his reputation during the last generation has risen high indeed.

In this all too brief study, I survey Middleton's career in Chapter 1 and discuss his nondramatic apprentice work in Chapter 2. Chapter 3 is concerned with comedies written for boys' companies; Chapter 4, with comedies done later; Chapter 5, with comedies on which Middleton collaborated. Chapter 6 is devoted to his tragicomedies; Chapter 7, to his masques and pageants; Chapter 8, to his tragedies. A final chapter briefly surveys Middleton criticism and assesses his achievements.

Limitations of space have unfortunately prevented all but cursory mention of several works of doubtful authorship, some of which may be Middleton's in whole or in part.

For this account of Middleton I owe a world of scholarly debts, the most of which I have acknowledged in the notes. I must, however, make two specific acknowledgments here: first, to Auburn University for a grant-in-aid given me several years ago; second, to the Folger Shakespeare Library and to Dr. Louis B. Wright, its former Director, for a fellowship which enabled me to study there in the summer of 1965. Finally, deepest thanks to my wife for enduring me, encouraging me, and helping me while I wrote.

NORMAN A. BRITTIN

*Auburn University*
*October, 1971*

# *Contents*

# *Chronology*

| | |
|---|---|
| 1580 | Thomas Middleton baptized April 18 at church of St. Lawrence in the Old Jewry, London. |
| 1586 | January 24, William Middleton, his father, buried; November 7, Anne, his mother, married Thomas Harvey. |
| 1597 | *The Wisdom of Solomon Paraphrased.* |
| 1598 | April, matriculated at Queen's College, Oxford. |
| 1599 | *Micro-cynicon.* |
| 1600 | *The Ghost of Lucrece.* |
| 1601 | February 8, in London, "accompaninge the players"; married Mary Marbeck. |
| 1602 | Writing plays for Philip Henslowe's companies. |
| *ca.* 1603 | Son Edward born. |
| 1604 | *The Ant and the Nightingale; or Father Hubburd's Tales. The Black Book.* Wrote speech of Zeal in *The Magnificent Entertainment* welcoming James I into London. |
| 1604–1606 | Writing plays for children's companies. |
| 1604 | February 20, Paul's Boys presented *The Phoenix* before King James. |
| 1606 | May 7, claimed to have delivered a play, *The Viper and Her Brood,* in payment of a debt. |
| *ca.* 1606–1607 | *Your Five Gallants* performed. |
| 1607 | Several plays entered for publication: *The Phoenix, Michaelmas Term, A Trick to Catch the Old One, The Family of Love.* |
| 1608 | *A Mad World, My Masters* entered for publication. |
| *ca.* 1608 | *The Roaring Girl* (with Dekker) performed. |
| 1609 | Living in Newington Butts. *Sir Robert Sherley Sent Ambassadour.* January 1, Children of Blackfriars per- |

formed *Trick* before the King. *Wit at Several Weapons* (with W. Rowley—and John Fletcher?) performed.

1608–1610 Difficulties over debts.

1612 *No Wit, No Help Like a Woman's* performed.

1613 September 29, *Running Stream Entertainment;* October 29, Lord Mayor's Show, *The Triumphs of Truth,* performed.

*ca.* 1613 *A Chaste Maid in Cheapside* performed.

1614 January 4, *The Masque of Cupid* (lost) performed.

*ca.* 1614 *The Witch* performed.

*ca.* 1615 *More Dissemblers Besides Women* performed.

*ca.* 1615–1617 *A Fair Quarrel* (with W. Rowley) performed.

1616 October 31, *Civitatis Amor* performed.

*ca.* 1616 *The Widow* performed.

1617 October 29, *The Triumphs of Honour and Industry* performed.

1618 *The Peacemaker.*

*ca.* 1618 *The Mayor of Queenborough* and *The Old Law* (with W. Rowley) performed.

1619 Between January 6 and February 2, *The Inner-Temple Masque* performed; October 29, *The Triumphs of Love and Antiquity* performed.

1620 *The Marriage of the Old and New Testament.* July 4, *The World Tost at Tennis* (with W. Rowley) performed. September 6, appointed city chronologer at £6/14/4 a year.

*ca.* 1620 *Anything for a Quiet Life* performed.

1621 *Honorable Entertainments.* January 23, salary as Chronologer raised to £10 a year. October 29, *The Sun in Aries* performed.

*ca.* 1621 *Women Beware Women* performed.

1622 *An Invention . . . for the . . . Lord Mayor. The Changeling* (with W. Rowley); October 29, *The Triumphs of Honour and Virtue* performed.

1621–1623 Recipient of various grants.

1623 *The Spanish Gipsy* (with Rowley—and John Ford?) performed.

1624 August, *A Game at Chess* performed.
1625 Engaged in preparations for official welcome of Charles I into London (abandoned because of plague).
1626 October 29, *The Triumphs of Health and Prosperity* performed.
1627 July 4, buried at Newington.
1628 July 18, his widow buried at Newington.

## CHAPTER 1

# *Thomas Middleton, Londoner*

THOUGH there exist many documents pertaining to Thomas Middleton, they tell us nothing, as is usual in his time, about the author's inner life; they inform us only about aspects of his public life which somehow were recorded in legal documents. But Middleton, most representative of Jacobean writers, after a professional career of a little less than thirty years covering the whole Jacobean age, left behind him at least twenty plays and probably more, several of which show exceptional powers of construction, satire, psychological penetration, and poetry.

It is appropriate that Middleton, who in his works reveals so much of the questioning and satirical Jacobean spirit, should have been born and reared in London, the sophisticated metropolis. His upbringing there was the most significant fact for his career.

### I *Family and Education*

Middleton was born in 1580 in Cheap Ward, the heart of the old walled city. His father, William, was a London bricklayer but a gentleman; for he had received a grant of arms in 1568. We do not know how old William was when in 1574 he married Anne Snow, a London woman more than thirty-five years of age. Apparently a prudent and prosperous man, William made himself more prosperous by purchasing leases of London property.[1] When he died in the winter of 1585–86, he was able to bequeath to his wife, his five-year-old son and his two-year-old daughter an estate of about three hundred and thirty-five pounds. The next June, following her late husband's advice, Anne Middleton conveyed the property in trust to three advisers so that she and her children were protected against possible selfishness or unscrupulousness on the part of a possible second husband.

Early in November, 1586, Anne Middleton remarried. Her new husband and the stepfather to her children was Thomas Harvey, a citizen and grocer of London, who appears to have been neither a steady nor a prosperous man but something of a rover, if not an adventurer. He had gone with the expedition under Sir Richard Grenville to plant Ralegh's colony on Roanoke Island, and he had invested his capital as "cape merchant"—chief factor—of the group. After a wretched year in America they returned to Plymouth on July 27, 1586. It seems likely that Harvey's wooing of Anne Middleton the next autumn was more for hope of gain than for love. Whether she, a woman nearing fifty, had been entirely frank with him about her fortunes, we cannot be sure; but his conduct certainly showed a persistent desire to gain control of the Middleton estate.

To judge by the records, Thomas Middleton's memories of his childhood and adolescence must have been given their special tinge by a mother who was far from young, a stepfather who disappeared from time to time, a great amount of parental strife, and more than a little family litigation. As soon as Thomas Harvey married and he discovered how his wife's property was held in trust, he became angry. There were legal strokes and counterstrokes in 1587, 1592, 1595, and 1599, during which we surmise that feelings were strained in the Harvey household. Harvey was away from England, however, at least three times during this period: in 1589 on the voyage against Portugal under Francis Drake and John Norris, in 1590 in the service of the queen in the Low Countries, and from late 1595 to 1599 at sea.

In 1598, Thomas Middleton's sister Avis married Allen Waterer, and strife broke out between Waterer and his mother-in-law. When Harvey returned in 1599, the struggle for the Middleton property was intensified by animosity between Waterer and Harvey. It seems probable that by the time he reached his majority Middleton had acquired considerable understanding of human rapacity, had decided that going to law profited chiefly the lawyers, and had perhaps been influenced in his views of military men by his stepfather, who described himself in a petition as "Captayne Thomas Harvey . . . sometyme a servitor both by land and Sea. . . ."

We do not know what grammar school Middleton attended,[2] but at eighteen, in 1598, he matriculated at Queen's College, Oxford, where he studied for more than two years;[3] but there is no record of his taking a degree. Perhaps he had difficulty in maintaining himself, or possibly "The Ant's Tale when he was a scholar" from *Father Hubburd's Tales* reveals a bit of Middleton's university experience. The ant tells of a student who came to the university with few clothes and only four books, and who was "slightly entertained to be a poor scholar and servitor to some Londoner's son, a pure cockney." While his master wasted his time on the tennis court, the poor scholar devoted himself early and late to Aristotle's logic; he had hopes of "future advancement" until he "was unfruitfully led to the lickerish study of poetry, that sweet honey-poison," [4] the practice of which led to his undoing.

We do know that Middleton was back in London in the summer of 1599, and perhaps in the summer of 1598, to help his mother with her troubles with Waterer and Harvey; that on December 3, 1599, he sold Waterer his half-share in his father's lease of Limehouse property; and that on the same day he sold Waterer his half-share in other properties for money "paid and disbursed for my advauncement & preferment in the vniuersity of Oxford where I am nowe a studient and for my maintenance with meat drincke and apparrell and other necessaries for me meet and convenient."

We next hear of Middleton from Anthony Snode, who testified on February 8, 1601, that "he remaynethe heare in London daylie accompaninge the players." Thus, after an abbreviated and not altogether satisfactory Oxford career, Middleton had left the university sometime between June 28, 1600, and February 8, 1601.

## II *The Professional Years*

After some early ventures in verse, Middleton—a belated University Wit, we might say—associated himself with the theater. Whatever "accompaninge the players" may mean, he was receiving during 1602 payments for his writing from Philip Henslowe, the theatrical magnate. We do not know what occasioned Middleton's connection with the theater, but sometime between 1601 and 1603 he married a woman whose brother Thomas Marbeck was in 1602 an actor with the Admiral's Men.[5] The earliest entry regarding Middleton in Henslowe's *Diary* records a payment to him and others for a play entitled *Caesar's Fall* (May 22, 1602). On October 3, Middleton was advanced one pound on a new play for the Earl of Worcester's Men; on October 21, he received four pounds in partial payment for *The Chester Tragedy* and two pounds more for it on November 9. (Six pounds was the regular rate of payment for a play at that time.) Henslowe also paid him five shillings for a prologue and an epilogue to Robert Greene's old *Friar Bacon and Friar Bungay* (*ca.* 1589), which was to have the honor of a court performance.[6]

The memorable year of 1603 saw the death of Queen Elizabeth, the accession of James I, and the ravages of the plague. Middleton's mother died in 1603, if not earlier; and plague struck his sister's family: one of her two daughters was buried on June 29, and her husband and their son were buried on July 15. On September 17, she married John Empson, a cutler, in Southwark. In 1603 or 1604 a son, Edward, was born to Middleton and his wife.

The plague of 1603 killed at least thirty thousand people in London alone, and the theaters were closed from shortly before May 17, 1603, until April 9, 1604. The players toured the provinces during the summer of 1603 and received "plentiful employment" from King James during the court's Christmas festivities. But 1603 must have been a hard year, economically, for players and playwrights.[7] Probably to eke out a precarious income Middleton wrote two satirical prose pamphlets printed in 1604, and helped Thomas Dekker with *1 Honest Whore*.[8] He also contributed one speech to *The Magnificent Entertainment,* the pageant that Dekker prepared as London's official welcome to the new ruler, King James.

From 1604 (if not earlier) to 1606, Middleton was writing comedies for children's companies, especially Paul's Boys. Sometime after July 30, 1606, Paul's Boys stopped playing; but in 1607 they published several plays they had bought from Middleton.

Fewer records have been discovered about Middleton's activities from this time on; but it seems likely from the evidence of borrowings and a lawsuit that he endured periods of struggle and debt.[9] By 1609 he had moved from the City to Newington Butts, a mile south of Southwark; and he lived the rest of his life there. A home in Newington would have been convenient to the theaters of the Bankside where certain of Middleton's plays were produced.

From 1613 on, Middleton was hired for many civic employments, chiefly the preparing of Lord Mayors' shows, which he sometimes produced as well as wrote. The accounts of the Worshipful Company of Grocers show that in 1617 the Grocers paid two hundred and eighty-two pounds "to Thomas Middleton, gent. for the ordering, overseeing, and writyng of the whole devyse, for the making of the Pageant of Nations, the Iland, the Indian Chariot, the Castle of Fame, . . . and for all the carpenter's work, paynting, guylding, and garnyshing of them, with all other things necessary for the apparelling and finding of all the personages in the sayd shewes,"[10] and for other details. In 1620 he was appointed Chronologer (Chronicler) of the City of London at a salary of £6 13*s.* 4*d.*, which was increased to ten pounds on January 23, 1621.[11]

With his civic employments and continuing work for the players, Middleton became a fairly well-to-do-man. During the middle and latter years of his career, he was a writer for the King's Men, and he created plays for the Prince's Men and for Lady Elizabeth's Men, especially in collaboration with William Rowley.

At some time in the course of his life Middleton became a chess player. The playing of chess is significant in one scene of *Women Beware Women,* and the idea of the opposing pieces on a chess board representing the opposition of the English-Protestant and the Spanish-Catholic is all-important in *A Game at Chess.* The play itself is unusual, and the effect of its production was unique in the history of English drama. Those who first saw it at the Globe on August 6, 1624, realized with joyous shock that the play truly set forth typical English hatred of Spain, their dislike of the Spanish Ambassador Count Gondomar, and their deep suspicion of the Catholics, especially of the Jesuits. Since nothing so topical had been permitted before (King James was opportunely away from the capital), word of this wonder of plays quickly spread, and the public crowded to see it, knowing it would not for long be available. To profit from its tremendous popularity, the King's Men, contrary to custom, played it day after day until it had had a run of nine days. Then the authorities closed it because of the vehement protests of Colonna, then Spanish ambassador—and a Catholic.

When the Privy Council ordered the author and the players to appear for examination, the players, who appeared on August 18, 1624, disclaimed any wrongdoing since the play had been licensed by the master of the revels. They were reprimanded (the official reason was the presentation on the stage of living Christian kings)[12] and were permitted to resume playing some ten days later only after giving assurance that they would not again present *A Game at Chess*. Middleton did not appear on August 18; and, when his son Edward was summoned for August 30, he could tell nothing of his father's whereabouts. Evidently, Middleton discreetly disappeared for a time. Since the performing of his *succès de scandale* was now prohibited, he made, or supervised the making of, various manuscript copies of it. Manuscripts were multiplied (five are still extant, more than of any other play of the period); and a few months later three surreptitiously printed quartos appeared.[13]

When King James died on March 27, 1625, the authorities of London planned an elaborate welcome to the city of the newly married Charles I, and Middleton was in charge of the affair. Triumphal arches had been erected and pageantry prepared, but the welcome had to be postponed on account of the plague, and finally it was given up. The authorities were not pleased with Middleton's achievement; and in January, 1626, the aldermen appointed an inspection committee because of a report "of abuses and badd workmanshipp." Although on June 8, 1626, Garret Christmas, Middleton's co-worker, was allowed to take the wagons apart and to keep the material, neither he nor Middleton was allowed further payment.[14]

Middleton's life was nearly over. He died not long after reaching his forty-seventh birthday and was buried at Newington on July 4, 1627. His wife petitioned the city for money on February 7, 1628, and was given twenty nobles. But she did not long outlive her husband; on July 18, 1628, she too was buried at Newington.

# CHAPTER 2

# *Ventures in Verse and Prose*

## I The Wisdom of Solomon Paraphrased

TRANSLATION or paraphrase of the Bible, such as Middleton's first published work, *The Wisdom of Solomon Paraphrased* (1597), was regarded in his time as a laudable occupation for a poet. Middleton would have considered his rendering into English verse of such hortatory material not only a commendable undertaking but also a test of the proficiency in verse-making that he had acquired by diligent exercise in composing Latin verses as well as an extended rhetorical effort providing the discipline that an apprentice poet requires. In this poem Middleton expanded the 429 verses of the Apocryphal *Wisdom of Solomon* into 705 six-line stanzas.

The injudicious length of paraphrase to which he committed himself, an elaboration of thought nearly tenfold, constituted a portentous challenge that he was ill-equipped to meet. He was not at the age of sixteen able to furnish real substance and attractive illustration. The result of his shortcomings is that criticism mentions *Wisdom Paraphrased* only to castigate it and Middleton as if he were "mature in dullness from his tender years." Swinburne, for example, called the poem a "tideless and interminable sea of limitless and inexhaustible drivel," and Bullen observed that it was "the most damnable piece of flatness that has ever fallen in my way." [1] But no critic has troubled to explain in precisely what cabinet of literary curiosities *Wisdom Paraphrased* should be classified.[2]

*The Wisdom of Solomon* itself is wholly admonitory and hortatory. If Middleton reflected on its lack of movement as a handicap to his success, however, he hoped to compensate for it by other attractions. Ironically, though *Wisdom Paraphrased* is almost synonymous with flatness and unreadability, Middleton intended it to be excessively brilliant; for such an exhibition of linguistic stunts, of rhetorical tumbling and contortion, has rarely been seen. The young author chose to write in the ornate, highly rhetorical manner that had been carried to such excesses by Shakespeare in *Venus and Adonis* and in *The Rape of Lucrece* and by Robert Southwell in *Saint Peter's Complaint.* The source of this style is in the long tradition of rhetorical exposition and practice stretching down from Greece of the fourth century B.C. and strongly maintained in grammar-school and university training of the sixteenth century.[3]

Of the 123 figures of rhetoric explained by George Puttenham in *The Arte of English Poesie,* Middleton used at least 48 in *Wisdom Paraphrased.* The rhetoric that fills and encrusts the poem is most apparent through the relatively few figures that Middleton oftenest employs. Most of all, he uses figures of contrast; for example, Antitheton—or antithesis, the bringing together of contraries—which we find at nearly every turn, is used with single words, phrases, couplets of successive stanzas, and even whole stanzas. He frequently uses Antimetabole, the repetition of a series of terms in reverse order: "Though eyes did stand in tears and tears in eyes" (290, XIX:3);[4] and Synoeciosis, the attribution of contrary qualities to a thing: "Poor and yet rich in fortune's overthrow" (154, II:10).

Middleton also makes use of Anaphora, beginning a series of verses with the same word (176–77, V:6); Ecphonisis, the figure of exclamation expressing emotions (144, I:4); and rhetorical questions. The rhetorical questions and particularly his massing them in one place, which is called Pysma, do much to give *Wisdom Paraphrased* its individual tone.

Single examples of Middleton's rhetoric fail to suggest the frequency and complexity with which in *Wisdom Paraphrased* he used figures; a single stanza often contains several of them.[5] A block of stanzas such as the first six of Chapter VII would well illustrate the quality of the poem and do justice to Middleton's love of word-play and to his use of rhetorical questions and exclamations. Antithesis had such an overwhelming attraction for Middleton that it often seems that no other way of developing his material suggested itself to him;[6] therefore, he swings back and forth, as on a tide, from one member of the antithesis to the other. These constant antitheses also emphasize paradoxes, in which he delighted with Elizabethan fervor.

"Light-arm'd with points, antitheses, and puns," *Wisdom Paraphrased* is vulnerable to criticism even if one were disposed to admire its rhetorical exuberance; for Middleton did not control his material well. Struggling for amplification and ornamentation, he overloaded his poem with rhetoric and now and again vitiated it by lack of control and by obviousness, tautology, and thinness of substance. Occasionally, however, he was capable of writing in a natural manner or could achieve poetry which, though certainly not great, deserves a modicum of praise.[7] He also showed poetic power by forming compound adjectives; and, as they appear increasingly toward the end of the poem, he evidently grew bolder and bolder in using these compounds. They reveal an imagination not without vigor and a mind fascinated by the possibilities of words but inclined to force them at times beyond their power.

## II The Ghost of Lucrece

In what was probably the next work Middleton wrote, though not the next to be published, *The Ghost of Lucrece*, he reworked the story Shakespeare had told in *The Rape of Lucrece;* and he used the same seven-line stanza Shakespeare had employed. In addition to reminiscences of Shakespeare's *Lucrece,* which we should expect to find, borrowings in *The Ghost of Lucrece* have been traced only to Greene's *Ciceronis Amor* (1589), from which Middleton took imagery, certain phrases, sententious statements, classical allusions, and even an idea or two.[8] Behind Middleton's poem, for which he adopted the form of a complaint (though with touches of the heroic epistle) lies a series of poems about women whose chastity was threatened.[9] In the complaint there appears a departed spirit to tell the poet the story of his life and especially of his downfall and wretched end. As Adams pointed out, Middleton did not retell the story of the rape of Lucrece by Tarquin (his poem has no plot), nor did he adhere strictly to the usual form of the complaint.[10] He departed from it in these respects: (1) at the beginning, the poet asks for Lucrece's ghost to be summoned; (2) the ghost does not dictate her story to the poet; (3) she speaks of using a pen, and toward the end she says she has written a letter to Tarquin. Thus Middleton blended the complaint with the heroic epistle.

His poem contains reproaches of Tarquin, an account of the purity of Lucrece and her maids, an allegorical summary of her tragedy, an attack on the vices of the age, and praise of chastity. Like Shakespeare's, the poem is full of "set pieces." Probably Middleton set himself not to imitate Shakespeare but to outdo him. Certainly the sharp attack on vice was unfamiliar material in a complaint. The satire on the immorality of the court seems, as Adams says,[11] to connect *The Ghost of Lucrece* with the new school of satire flourishing in 1598–99.

*The Ghost of Lucrece* is less rhetorical than *Wisdom Paraphrased.* However, exclamations, strained metaphors, rhetorical questions, and plays on words produce much turgid writing. The style of Middleton's first two works seems chiefly notable for its sense of sweaty strain. His verbal arabesques are products of one who had had little experience of life and who had not advanced beyond a grammar-school vein. These poems are two of the last examples of Elizabethan stylistic exuberance, for it was to be superseded later by the more realistic, biting, and critical Jacobean style.[12] In fact, Shakespeare's Holofernes in *Love's Labour's Lost* (IV.ii.125–27) had already provided an appropriate comment for Middleton's work: "Here are only numbers ratified; but, for the elegancy, facility, and golden cadence of poetry, *caret.*"

## III Micro-cynicon

Evidently Middleton's unversity studies did not prevent his giving attention to contemporary literature, for in 1599 a volume of his poems, *Micro-cynicon. Sixe Snarling Satyres,* reflects the satiric trend of the era. Satires became especially popular following the publication in 1597 of Joseph Hall's *Virgidemiarum,* a volume containing three books of "toothless satires," which was completed in 1598 by "Three last Bookes of Byting Satyres." Sensing the changing temper of the times, Middleton joined the satirical chorus, most of them young men who were vying with the Romans by using more or less the fashion of the Classical satire which they transposed into the key of the English heroic couplet, with which Edmund Spenser had led the way in *Mother Hubberds Tale* (1591). They were also vying with one another, for all complained about much the same abuses.

The sixteenth century was an age of change and unsettledness; of abuses, unfairness, oppression; and above all—many people thought—of sin. Decade after decade—the voice of complaint rising to a crescendo in the closing years of the century—the preacher, moralist, and satirist attacked the evils of the times and tried to show the epoch its own ugly and unwilling face in the stern glass of truth. Though many of its blemishes were old, some were new: medieval patterns of culture were breaking up, individualism was growing, the middle class was gaining power, an inchoate capitalism was shocking people by its cold-bloodedness and greed, enclosures were driving farmers off the land, rents were rising, prices were increasing, and venality was rampant everywhere but especially in London.[13]

The moral purpose of Elizabethan satire is unmistakable; the satirists insist on their serious responsibility and their moral intent. But the authorities of the Tudor state were thin skinned, and *Micro-cynicon* did not circulate long. Soon after its publication, the Archbishop of Canterbury and the Bishop of London commanded the destruction of several volumes of satires and forbade the publication of any more satires or epigrams (*Stationers' Register,* June 1, 1599). "Presently therevppon," Middleton's *Snarling Satires* were burnt—along with books by Hall, John Marston, and Edward Guilpin— according to the *Stationers' Register* (June 4, 1599).

Middleton doubtless got from Hall's "Byting Satyres" the suggestion for his subtitle "Sixe Snarling Satyres," and he also followed Hall in prefacing his work with "His Defiance to Envy." Marston's vehement type of satire is Middleton's model in his "Author's Prologue" and in satires I and V. Like Marston, Middleton feels that satire is meant to scourge vice, and he begins his first satire by conventionally deploring the fact that the age has fallen away from truth and into sin: "But, O destruction of our latter days!/How much from verity this age estrays/Ranging the briery deserts of black sin" (117). But he does not maintain the constant lashing of sin; and some of his satires are not in Marston's high-pitched, ill-tempered, declamatory strain. Middleton's work deviates into character sketches, scenes from London life, and little narratives. By this time English poets, who had done a fair amount of experimenting with formal satire, were moving farther away each year from Classical models, and Middleton's *Micro-cynicon* represents the furthest remove from direct Classical imitation that English satire had reached by 1599. For, in it, English elements of style, narrative, and local color emphatically predominate over the Classical elements.[14]

In satires I and II, Middleton attacks avarice and extravagance, and in Satire III, "Insolent Superbia," he turns to pride. But, in the main, the poem is an attack upon women; and, only so far as women are proud, is it an attack upon pride. Middleton's character Superbia describes in detail the setting of a sumptuous feast she has just had, and she presents a convincing picture of London life. After a rhetorical passage admonishing women, the author presents another scene—one more realistic and dramatic than the account of the feast,—in which "fine madam Tiptoes," full of haughtiness, vents her ill-nature on her maid. This lively little scene has scant satiric effect, for Middleton has became so interested in his characters that one tends to appreciate the vividness with which Superbia's idiosyncrasy is rendered rather than to resent the idiosyncrasy.

Satire IV is a versified conny-catching tale rather than a satire. In fluent couplets Middleton tells of Cheating Droone, who, having found in St. Paul's a rich, unsuspecting gull, orders a feast for the gentleman; keeps him late at the tavern with talk, music, and more wine; and, when the gentleman is dead drunk, puts him to bed and robs him of ten pounds. In this tale—told with colloquial, Chaucerian ease—one finds Middleton's first use of the gullery that often appears in his city comedies. He has so relished the tale that he remembers to give only a little moralizng flick with the satiric lash: "Be wise, young heads, care for an after-day!" (127–30).

Considering the rhetoric and turgidity of Middleton's earlier poetry and judging his "satires" as points in his poetic development, the reader is likely to feel that the young author was improving in *Micro-cynicon,* that he was showing an unsuspected versatility in handling aspects of the life about him, and that his style was far from lacking skill. His arriving at anything like a vernacular style, considering his earlier poems, is indeed a small triumph; but here one becomes aware for the first time in his career of sharp observation of real life. The easy, vivid writing of satires III and IV is very good; and satire IV, the conny-catching tale, not only has the greatest ease and rapidity of versification but also shows Middleton experimenting in a narrative line different from that of the other satirists.[15] This poem has a distinctly Chaucerian ring; only from *The Canterbury Tales* could Middleton have learned to tell a rogue tale as he tells "Cheating Droone."

Though still leaning heavily upon others, Middleton had at last begun to look sharply at the London about him and to apply his vivid, barely restrained imagination to the task of reproducing in verse what he saw. He had put a tentative foot on the road he was to follow.

## IV *Two Satirical Pamphlets*

Middleton's early satirical pamphlets, mainly in prose, *The Black Book* (1604) and *Father Hubburd's Tales: or, The Ant and the Nightingale* (1604),[16] show his advance along the route of realism. The pamphlets had their inception in works by Robert Greene and Thomas Nashe. Greene had promised in his *Disputation between a He-cony catcher and a She-cony catcher* (1592) to put out something entitled *The Blacke Booke,* in which he would continue his exposures of scoundrels, but Greene died and no *Blacke Booke* appeared.[17] Though the title and to some extent the subject matter of Middleton's *Black Book* related to Greene's work, its framework was suggested by Nashe's *Pierce Penilesse His Supplication to the Divell* (1592). In this work, Pierce, the poor scholar, supplicates the devil for an opportunity to obtain gold; and he finally finds a Knight of the Post (a professional perjurer) who says he is the devil's man and will deliver Pierce's letter. Nashe said in the second edition that he might presently write about the return of the Knight of the Post with the devil's answer; and, though he did not do so, three replies were written in the early seventeenth century, and the first of these was Middleton's *Black Book.*[18]

Middleton introduced the pamphlet with a disarming piece of irony, "The Epistle to the Reader," which is half scornful and half serious—probably the product of his chagrin over the burning of *Micro-cynicon* by the hangman. Issuing another satirical work (possibly a violation of the order of June 1, 1599, if it were to be strictly enforced), the young author offers a straightfaced explanation "To all those that are truly virtuous, and can touch pitch and yet never defile themselves. . . ." He announces, with the satirist's usual justification, that his labors have a "wholesome intent"; and he concludes that "no virtuous spirit or judicial worthy but will approve my politic moral, where, under the shadow of the devil's legacies, or his bequeathing to villains, I strip their villanies naked, and bare the infected bulks of craft, cozenage, and panderism, the three bloodhounds of a commonwealth" (5-6).

In the pamphlet proper, Lucifer himself comes to earth in various disguises.[19] He finds out where Pierce Penilesse lives in dirt and squalor and he tells him that, moved by his petition, he has come to relieve his poverty. Then Lucifer, as a usurer, goes to the Royal Exchange; and, in a captain's suit, he visits Bezle's ordinary to dice with conny-catchers. Finally he dictates his will to a scrivener (33). His heirs are the pander, thief, catchpoll, cheating bowler, cutpurse, and dice player. Lucifer then departs for Hell.

Middleton has been inculcating a moral lesson by humorous means—identifying the devil's intimates who carry on his business. He uses a particular satirical *genre,* the mock testament. As far back as the fourth century, the mock testament provided a wicked opportunity of satirizing the vices or shortcomings of the legatees, and it became a very popular form of burlesque in the late Middle Ages.[20] A prose variation of the form, an anonymous *Wyll of the Deuyll and his Last Testament,*[21] is almost certainly Middleton's model.

The chief purpose of these testaments is to satirize certain groups. In *The Wyll of the Deuyll* bequests are made to Papists, deceiving tradesmen, ruffians, dice players, usurers, lawyers, women, fornicators, and hypocrites. Middleton's satire is directed against sharpers and criminals (save for Pierce and a tobacco-taker) of the sort that appear in conny-catching pamphlets; however, the legatees are more individualized than those of his model; and his style is wittier, with plenty of word play. But his attacks are not savage; the wit mollifies the satire.

Middleton writes about London life in the style of Nashe, the virtuoso of satirical burlesque whose style is characterized by humorous exaggeration and caricature, by occasional use of harsh and sordid details relieved by the gusto with which the author enjoys them, by vividness of phrasing, by surprising similes and metaphors, and by unabashed word play. Nashe adopted an anti-heroic attitude and a conversational tone; and, like Rabelais and other Renaissance writers, he admired verbal ingenuity and abundance.[22] Middleton imitated Nashe's way of writing prose because the style was congenial to his spirit, and because Middleton explicitly admitted his admiration for Nashe in the poetical introduction to *Father Hubburd's Tales:* "Thy name they bury, having buried thee;/Drones eat thy honey—thou wert the true bee" (63). A fair example of Middleton's Nashe-like writing is his picture of the lieutenant in the bawdy house of *The Black Book* (13–14). From such a caricature and from the description of Pierce Penilesse's chamber (25–26) one may appreciate the fertility of Middleton's imagination and the sharpness of his observation which combine to produce pungent similes. In such similes based upon ordinary London experience, Middleton outshone Nashe. His prose differs, however, from Nashe's (and Dekker's) in being almost free of Latin quotations.

Middleton's other pamphlet, *The Ant and the Nightingale,* but better known as *Father Hubburd's Tales,* contains three tales told in prose by the ant but with introductory and intercalary material in verse.[23] Upon hearing that the ant had formerly been a man, the nightingale invites him to tell his story. He tells first of his bitter experience as a plowman after the death of his old landlord. As soon as the old landlord died, "the bell might well have tolled for hospitality, and good housekeeping." The young heir soon calls the tenants to London and tells them he is going to give them leases for years instead of the old type of holding by which they might have been turned out without notice. A lawyer, a mercer, and a merchant ("to whom he [the son] was much beholding") are to arrange matters.

At the meeting, the ways of the city are shown through the unsophisticated eyes of the countrymen. Crowds await the lawyer, offer him gold, do him submission as if he were God. To the tenants, he mentions "fines" in every sentence—"but that word *fines* was no fine word, me thought, to please poor labouring husbandmen, that can scarce sweat out so much in a twelve-month as he would demand in a twinkling." Their young master arrives, "metamorphosed into the shape of a French puppet" with new-fangled clothes that had cost more than two years' rent. The labourers perceive that the mercer and merchant "had fitted my young master in clothes, whilst they had clothed themselves in his acres." To obtain more cash, the heir is obliged to sign over to the City men all his interest in his estate.[24] Feeling that the world is turned upside down, the plowmen are told by their new masters that they must pay such fines as the lawyer shall proportion to them. The lawyer requires them to return the next quarter, and he tells the prodigal heir how to live a life of fashion and extravagance in the city. The prodigal goes off with a débauché, squanders his money on a "most delicate drab," and soon turns conny-catcher and pimp: "He was all that might be in dissolute villany, and nothing that should be in his forefathers' honesty" (67, 68, 71, 77, 79, 85). Middleton ends the tale fantastically by turning the plowmen back into ants.

In this tale Middleton exposes one of the most troublesome problems of sixteenth-century England—the land question, which was related, as he shows, to usury, extravagance, and prostitution. Ever since the monastery lands had been confiscated, tradesmen of London had been acquiring land. According to feudal law, a tenant was liable to pay a fine (a fee in addition to his rent) upon alteration in the tenancy or upon renewal of a lease. Thus the City men, having taken over an estate (and greased the lawyer's palm), were able to levy fines upon the plowmen. The next scene in the story, if Middleton had continued it, would have been the raising of the tenants' rents. The taking of interest was still considered to be usury, an object of continuous censure throughout the Middle Ages, in the Elizabethan period, and down into the seventeenth century. Nevertheless, usury increased. Middleton, though born and reared in the City, attacks usury; and his narrative about the plowman reveals his understanding of the relationship between landlords and money-lenders. He is in sympathy with the tenants, and his presenting of the situation through the country men's eyes is an effective device to contrast the old-fashioned (country) virtues and the new (city) vices.[25]

The second tale, in which the ant tells of experiences in the army, reflects the same social concern. Although writing in the flippant and ingenious manner of Nashe, Middleton reveals the hardships of Elizabethan soldiers, who suffered because their pay was always in arrears, their officers were corrupt, and the society to which they returned felt small responsibility for them. Middleton's soldier, "lurched" of right arm and leg, found himself dismissed with one month's pay for ten months' service. He bitterly implies that he was simply thrown out, crippled as he was, to beg or die. Finally, to avoid going to jail, he turns himself back into an ant (90, 93–94, 96, 97).

Yet the powers of the kingdom were not completely callous regarding the soldiers' plight; a society fearful of uprising groped toward fairly humane treatment of its old soldiers. In 1601 Parliament provided for pensions to be paid to those wounded or crippled in war; but any veteran taken begging after the following Easter was to lose his pension forever and be treated as a common rogue.[26] The wealthy and powerful upholders of stability who regarded unfixed persons with so much hostility might congratulate themselves that they had cared handsomely for old soldiers; but Middleton shows himself as not on the side of the wealthy and powerful but as on that of the soldier who considered himself unappreciated and abused.

The ant tells his third tale about his experiences as a scholar. "A needy scholar!" the nightingale exclaims: "worse than worst,/Less fate in that than both the first. . . ." The ant tells the story, already related (in Chapter 1 of this book) of how he goes to the university, poorly provided, as a servitor to a Cockney student. Having succumbed to the "sweet honey-poison" of poetry and having created "an elaborate poetical building," he has a copy bound in vellum, adorned with gold-leaf, "strung most gentleman-like with carnation silk riband," and presents it to one Sir Christopher Clutchfist. But, when he visits his patron, hoping for a reward, he is dismayed to find the cover ripped off the book, and the carnation strings in the knight's Spanish leather shoes. After falling into a swoon, he awakes as an ant (104–7).

This third tale was added to Middleton's volume in the second edition, which also carries a dedication "to the true general patron of all Muses, Musicians, Poets, and Picture-drawers, Sir Christopher Clutchfist." Middleton addresses him insultingly by calling him "most guerdonless sir, pinching patron, and the Muses' bad paymaster" (51). The savage abuse of this ironic dedication, the likeness of its details to those of the ant's third tale, and the fact that they are particularly lifelike and specific led J. Q. Adams to believe that Middleton was attacking Lord Compton, to whom he had dedicated *The Ghost of Lucrece*. Adams's suggestion is possibly correct: it is psychologically plausible, for it fits in with Middleton's situation. All through his early work one finds an interest in money, the would-be disdainful interest of the poor but talented young gentleman who is half disgusted, half envious when he sees money in the hands of those he considers less worthy than himself.

*Father Hubburd's Tales* is written much like *The Black Book*, but with slightly less verve; however, in content, the first two tales show a deeper social interest. In prose, Middleton holds his own with Nashe and Dekker; he has an abundant fund of word play, simile, sarcasm, and humor—a swift and sprightly way of writing.

Looking back over Middleton's early nondramatic works,[27] one is likely to be most impressed by his experimentation. He has tried highly rhetorical poetry; he has tried satire, both in verse and in prose; he has played the "sedulous ape" to several writers; and he has done his best writing when imitating the fashion of Chaucer and of Nashe, both realists. He has found it difficult to control his imagination; he has a dangerous tendency toward overadornment. He has always followed a pattern that someone else else has created; but he has filled it with details of his own. Satire seems to come naturally to him; and, to support it, he has a gift for observing details and is acquiring a considerable knowledge of the world about him. He has moved further and further toward popular forms of literature; and, because he possesses, in addition to his literary talent, the gift of adaptability, he will succeed.

## CHAPTER 3

# *Comedies for the Boys' Companies*

AT the beginning of Middleton's career as a comic dramatist, he found congenial dramatic antecedents for imitation in the recent and popular comedies of George Chapman, Ben Jonson, Marston, and Dekker, who emphasized "humours" and satire. Shakespeare had had successes with middle-class and lower-class characters in *Henry IV*, *Henry V*, and *The Merry Wives of Windsor*;[1] and Middleton's friend Dekker had provided in *The Shoemakers' Holiday* an example of romantic action mingled with a realistic portrayal of London tradesfolk. As for nondramatic antecedents, Middleton had experience in creating the "characters" of formal satire; and he was also familiar with the conny-catching pamphlets of Greene.[2] At first, Middleton reveals an allegiance to declining Elizabethan romance mingled with the attraction of the new Jacobean critical spirit; but he soon becomes a complete Jacobean.[3] His earliest independent comedies were produced by Paul's Boys, an *avant-garde* group that appealed to fashionable tastes, and especially to the current taste for satire. For several years Middleton was aligned with this new "coterie drama."[4] The best of these "city comedies" give him much of his reputation as a comic dramatist.

### I The Phoenix

*The Phoenix* is one of the earliest of Middleton's extant plays. If, as seems likely, he aimed the play directly at new King James as both a compliment and a suggestion, he probably composed it late in 1603.[5] The unifying action of *The Phoenix* is a disguise plot, one similar in essentials to that of Shakespeare's *Measure for Measure*.[6] In the action, the Duke of Ferrara, nearing death after ruling for forty-five years, follows Proditor's suggestion to send Prince Phoenix traveling. Proditor wants the prince out of the way so that he himself can seize power. But Phoenix disguises himself and with his servant Fidelio remains at home to learn about corruptions that may have developed during his father's too lenient reign. The Prince makes a little circle of Ferrara, as it were, and at several points on the circle he encounters vice and crime. The play shows his exposure and his punishment of the evildoers.

In Middleton's comedies, generally, the subsidiary action tends to present the activities of several characters who are related in some way to the characters of the main plot, but often only in a casual way, perhaps only by acquaintance. Many scenes are really independent, but Middleton's technique supplies them with a specious unity. The scenes follow each other so rapidly and are so dramatically effective that, as Dunkel says, they carry the reader "along to the conclusion with increasing interest." [7]

These comments apply to the five different actions of *The Phoenix,* which are introduced in the first act and which proceed almost as driftingly as a "slice-of-life" novel. But all the characters save the Captain (disposed of in Act II) are given a reason for coming to court in the last act; and there they receive their due. Around the whole play is thrown the idea that the city suffers from corruption. To balance this corrupt situation, Middleton supplies the unifying idea of reformation, which Prince Phoenix succeeds in bringing about.

The corruptions of Ferrara are, of course, the corruptions of England as the realistic, satirical writers of the time saw them: abuses of justice, rampant litigiousness, the lusts of city wives, the extravagance and debauchery of courtiers, and the rapacity of lawyers. Various suggestions for the benefit of King James are set forth, as when Phoenix says: "So much have the complaints and suits of men, seven, nay, seventeen years neglected, still interposed by coin and great enemies, prevailed with my pity, that I cannot otherwise think but there are infectious dealings in most offices, and foul mysteries throughout all professions. . . . For oft between kings' eyes and subjects' crimes/Stands there a bar of bribes . . ." (I.i. 105–19). Later in a well-known apostrophe to "thou angel sent amongst us, sober Law" (I.iv. 197 ff.), Phoenix deplores the abuses of justice at the lower levels of jurisdiction and pleads for quick and fair consideration for the common man.

The investigations of Phoenix are probably intended as object-lessons to King James: "indeed, a prince need no[t] travel farther than his own kingdom, if he apply himself faithfully . . ." (I.i.

90–95). Phoenix believes: "That king stands sur'st who by his virtue rises/More than by birth or blood"; and Fidelio rejoins: "Who labours to reform is fit to reign./How can that king be safe that studies not/The profit of his people?" (I.i. 130–31; 137–39). Similar complimentary suggestions appear also in Act V. Middleton apparently hoped that James would be pleased by the parallel between himself and the diligent, incorruptible new ruler Phoenix, eager to reform after the reign of his father, who, like Queen Elizabeth, had ruled for forty-five years but perhaps too mildly—"For there's as much disease, though not to th' eye,/In too much pity as in tyranny" (I.i. 9–10).

Most of the characters of *The Phoenix* are little more than flat types whose qualities are suggested by their names. The Duke and Phoenix are conventional rulers of good intention, and the Prince is a young man whose speeches are consistently delivered in a stiffish, moralizing fashion. Proditor (Latin, *traitor*) is the conventional plotter against the throne, Fidelio is ever faithful, and Castiza ever chaste. Although these names reveal how *The Phoenix* is related to the comedy of "humours," Tangle is the most thoroughly "humourous" of the characters; for his passion for litigation masters him and sweeps him through fanaticism into madness. When Quieto cures him by a blood letting,[8] all the law terms that so fevered him spurt forth in a "filthy stream of trouble, spite, and doubt" (V.i. 308).

The conventionality of the characters shows, too, that Middleton was more interested in the ideas they represent (particularly in relation to the state of society) and in their more or less mechanical manipulation from one scene to another than he was in complexities of their being or in the subtleties of their souls. Although one cannot, for example, mention in the same breath Proditor and Shakespeare's Angelo, three of Middleton's characters do possess human warmth and vigor. The first is the Captain, a swaggerer, a cad, and something of a conny-catcher, who would prey on the "venturer" unlucky enough to back his voyage. Though on a lower level of society, he is related to Sir Petronel Flash of *Eastward Ho.* Mean and callous, the Captain is a realistically drawn rogue and not an abstraction. The second character is Falso's daughter, who, if she had a name, would probably be called Lascivia; she is the first representative in Middleton's work of wanton city wives. But her bold assurance, the strength of her desires, and her social aspirations give her considerable individuality. The third character is Justice Falso himself.

Falso, a considerable comic triumph, is the most memorable character of the play. The rogue is doubtless somewhat indebted to Falstaff for his quick wit, his effrontery, and his logic-chopping. But, a Falstaff transposed into another key, Falso is no mere copy, and he is not just an abstraction; neither is he a drily realistic portrait of some actual justice, though he is individualized. Indeed, as Miss Ellis-Fermor has observed, even Fielding need not have been ashamed of Falso.[9] When the shrewd old villain soliloquizes on the tingling excitement of his youthful adventures as a highwayman, one seems to see the very life of the man:

> I have been a youth myself: I ha' seen the day I could have told money out of other men's purses,—mass, so I can do now,—nor will I keep that fellow about me that dares not bid a man stand; for as long as drunkenness is a vice, stand is a virtue: but I would not have 'em taken. I remember now betimes in a morning, I would have peered through the green boughs, and have had the party presently, and then to ride away finely in fear: 'twas e'en venery to me, i'faith, the pleasantest course of life! one would think every woodcock a constable, and every owl an officer. But those days are past with me; and a' my troth, I think I am a greater thief now, and in no danger (III.i.64–71).

The corruption in Ferrara is signalized by the fact that Falso, a cynical bribe-taker and protector of robbers, is a justice of the peace who openly states his professional philosophy: "I think it a great spark of wisdom and policy, if a man come to me for justice, first to know his griefs by his fees, which be light, and which be heavy; he may counterfeit else, and make me do justice for nothing: I like not that; for when I mean to be just, let me be paid well for't: the deed so rare purges the bribe" (I.vi. 50–56).

Against this depravity—which also includes the treason of Proditor, the cynicism of Proditor and the Captain, the lust of Falso, and the lechery of his daughter—the honorable characters stand out in contrast: Phoenix and Fidelio, Castiza, Falso's niece, and Quieto. The Prince's denunciations of city wives, gambling, extravagance, and the land problem accord with *Micro-cynicon* and *Father Hubburd's Tales.* By emphasizing contemporary dishonesty, greed, and depravity, Middleton implies that in the past society was better; thus, Middleton, the satirist-moralist, like all such writers, advocates by implication an antique simplicity and uprightness.

## II The Family of Love

*The Family of Love* was composed before October 12, 1607, when Sir George Buc licensed it for printing—and perhaps considerably earlier, for the author remarked in a note "To the Reader" that it was published "too late, for that it was not published when the general voice of the people had sealed it for good, and the newness of it made it much more desired than at this time. . . ." How long a time intervened between production and printing one has no way of knowing, but the style in the romantic plot seems uncharacteristic of Middleton; and, if he wrote the romantic part of the play, it seems reasonable to think of *Family* as an early work written while he was still experimenting with styles.[10]

Published anonymously, *Family* was attributed to Middleton by Edward Archer in 1656; and this attribution was accepted without question until challenged by Gerald J. Eberle in 1948. Basing his argument on internal evidence—chiefly alleged parallels with Dekker's work—Eberle asserted that the text "is a revision by Dekker and Middleton of an early play written by Middleton with considerable help from Dekker." [11] Eberle's contention has, however, not been accepted because his thesis is so complex and because his methodology is faulty.[12]

If Dekker's name had originally been assigned to the play, however, it seems likely that it would readily have been added to the canon of his work. The comedy deals with a favorite Dekker theme, the victory of a pair of romantic lovers over mercenary opposition; it imitates *Romeo and Juliet* and borrows from other plays of Shakespeare (Dekker often imitates Shakespeare); it has likenesses to *Westward Ho!* and *Northward Ho!* (by Dekker and Webster); and it contains numerous Classical allusions of the sort Dekker used. The blank verse is more wooden than that of Middleton's *The Phoenix,* and terms such as "Bright Phoebus' steeds" (I.ii.100), "Elysium's sweet" (II.iv.36), "Argus' wakeful eyes" (III.i.1), "Phitonessa's power" (III.vii.5), and "Indian mines and Tagus' glistering ore" (V.iii.448), as well as the Classical allusions poured out at the beginning and end of Act IV, Scene ii, do not appear in Middleton's other dramas.

Richard Levin, however, has pointed out that the construction of *Family* resembles that in other Middleton plays, especially *A Chaste Maid in Cheapside* (*ca.* 1613). He suggests that the incongruities of style derive from the differing qualities of the three-level action (farce, realistic satire, and romance) and from the young author's inability to pitch correctly the romantic tone in the love scenes of his main plot.[13] Even if Dekker wrote parts of the play, the firm plotting is evidently Middleton's.

In the main plot, the hopes of a pair of true romantic lovers, Gerardine and Maria, are thwarted by Maria's avaricious guardian, Dr. Glister, who declares: "Wealth commands all" (III.ii.108). He forbids Maria to marry Gerardine, who, he says, is an inconstant gallant; and he locks her in her chamber. Gerardine announces that he will leave England since he has failed to win Maria; but, after arousing Mrs. Glister's jealousy regarding her husband and Maria, Gerardine finds means to get into Maria's room; and there they live together in secret.

Rebecca Purge, the chief character in the satirical subplot, is a member of the Family of Love, an Anabaptist sect. According to Sir John Harington's Epigram 374, these Familists were so assured of being among the elect that they felt that their sinning would carry no penalty:

> One of the foolish family of love
> That of their sure election stand so glorious
> They think that ev'n their sinns are meritorious,
> Did earst a sister to his pleasure move,
> Alleadging, sith no sinn their soules could taint,
> They might begett som prophett or a saint.[14]

It is ironical that this female precisian Rebecca, who cannot endure organs in church or bear to hear organs of the body mentioned, should be Glister's mistress and have carnal adventures in the meetings of the Family. She is also pursued by Lipsalve and Gudgeon; and she is watched by her jealous husband, the apothecary. Lipsalve and Gudgeon, "two gallants that only pursue city lechery," plot to gain the favors of any available woman—first Maria, then Mrs. Purge, and finally Mrs. Glister. They are treated farcically in the episodes where they appear.

Both Gerardine and Maria assert the purity, constancy, and divine origin of their love. After she becomes pregnant, he leaves to arrange additional details of his scheme; and Mrs. Glister becomes bitterly jealous of and angry with her husband, whom she supposes to be guilty of adultery. With the aid of the sympathetic merchant Dryfat, Gerardine gets all the parties summoned to Dryfat's house, where Mrs. Purge and Dr. Glister are accused of incontinence. In a lively mock-trial Gerardine, disguised as Dr. Stickler, hands down decisions that lead to a happy ending.

Levin's analysis of the play reveals the hierarchical pattern of the three actions that comprise the plot. The lustful gallants are treated farcically, being given physical punishments by Dr. Glister; but Dr. Glister, who is hypocritically engaged with the Purges and other middle-class characters on the second level, is outwitted and given his punishment through social criticism and his purse by Gerardine. Gerardine, the controller of the play, determines the outcome of all three actions. He and Maria represent a real "family of love"—and one distinctly above the sordid designs and values of the others.[15]

Since the characters rarely spring to life, the main interest of the play lies in plot and satire. The satire is directed against the mercenary attitudes of the uncle-guardian of the heroine, the indiscriminate lust of the gallants, and especially the hypocrisy of the Puritans. Middleton presents the meetings of the Family of Love as a means of concealing immorality but does not show the Familists as any different from other Puritans, whom dramatists in general satirized for their uncharitable spirit and for their narrow adherence to the letter of a religion that emphasized trivialities of speech and conduct. The comedy does not suggest a whole society pervaded by vice, as does *The Phoenix;* but the mock-trial is rather like the court-ensemble scene at the close of *The Phoenix* in which the Prince dispenses appropriate penalties.

## III Your Five Gallants

Middleton reverted to the technique of *The Phoenix* in *Your Five Gallants,* that was most likely staged in 1607.[16] A play based on the exposure of crime and vice, its plot is motivated through the choosing of one of the gallants as a husband by Katherine, a wealthy orphan. The five gallants are really "caterpillars" in the commonwealth, though each dresses, and bears himself, as a gentleman. Their names hint at their occupations: Frippery, a pawnbroker: Primero, a bawd; Goldstone, a cheater; Pursenet, a cutpurse and highway robber; and Tailby, the whore-gallant, a favorite of women. When Katherine tells her suitors that in one month she will announce her choice, the month is used by Fitsgrave, her sixth suitor and an honorable gentleman, to discover the hidden truth about the other five and to prepare for their exposure, which comes in the fifth act.

The play strikes a strong picaresque note, for it exhibits much trickery, duplicity, and baseness among the "gallants," who conceal the sordid reality of their lives behind a façade of fashionably dissolute gentility. It presents lively realistic scenes which, one suspects, seemed to many of the young gentlemen who frequented private theaters to be a candid reflection of contemporary manners. Act I opens on Frippery carefully refusing pawns from parishes where plague-deaths have been reported; Act II shows the gallants dicing at the Mitre; in Acts I and III there are scenes at Primero's bawdy house; Act IV has a table set for dinner at the house of a rich merchant; and the dénouement occurs in a masque in Act V.

*Your Five Gallants* makes use of various disguises, chief among which is the disguise of Fitsgrave as Bouser, "a credulous scholar" fresh from the university, to whom the others are glad to show the dissipation of the big city. Plot activity is also provided by the changing possession of a chain of pearls, which in each act comes into the hands of at least one different person. Because of their contention over the pearls, the five gallants are all revealed to each other. Laughing, they agree that the one to marry Katherine "shall bear himself more portly . . . / . . . and be a countenance to the rest" (IV.viii.250–51). This situation, as Goldstone sees himself plotting for them all, reminds one of Falso's arrangements in *The Phoenix*. But Goldstone has the idea that they should be presented to Katherine "in a strange-gallant and conceited masque" for which Bouser, the scholar, is to provide the device.

Fitsgrave prepares their shields, each with suitable emblems and Latin mottoes; when he mistranslates the Latin for them during their rehearsal, they are all pleased. For example, Pursenet's device is "a purse wide open, and the mouth downward: the word, *Alienis ecce crumenis! . . . One that lives out of other men's pockets.*" But Pursenet is told that it means "*Your bounty pours itself forth to all men*" (V.i.88–92, 148).[17] The dénouement is accomplished by means of the conventional dramatic contrivance of the masque at Katherine's house, where Fitsgrave points out the sordid realities of the gallants' lives. For punishment, Pursenet's thieving boy and Primero are to be whipped; the others must marry the courtesans who are revealed as shield-boys in the masque. Katherine, of course, chooses Fitsgrave for her husband.

One could imagine Middleton in the period when he wrote this play as digging into conny-catching pamphlets in order to find picaresque material to be dramatized. Goldstone and Fulk substitute a pair of false beakers for real ones at the Mitre, cheat with false dice, and steal a gilt goblet by concealing it and inducing the gallants to pay for it rather than endure searching and gossip. The last to leave, they take it along. These and other methods of cheating of Goldstone and Pursenet, revelations of the underworld similar to some of the material in *The Black Book*, are taken from pamphlets of the period.[18]

*Your Five Gallants* is a clean-cut, satirical exposure of city sharpers; Fitsgrave is the honest man who out-tricks them. One might call it a play on impudence: Goldstone's remark: "What cannot wit, so it be impudent,/Devise and compass?" (IV.viii. 55–56) represents the attitude that Middleton satirizes; it might well be taken as the motto of some of his heroes in other plays. But here he is writing a highly moral play and inveighing against the evils of the age in the typical satirist's manner.

## IV A Mad World, My Masters

*A Mad World, My Masters* (*ca.* 1607) has a lively intrigue plot. In the main action, Follywit, prankish leader of a gang of rogues, invents projects to fleece his grandfather, Sir Bounteous Progress. Sir Bounteous has resolved that, though Follywit is to be his heir, not a penny is to go to the young man until after the grandfather's death. Yet, ironically, Sir Bounteous takes immense pride in being the most bountiful dispenser of hospitality in his shire. While the main plot concerns Follywit's campaign against his grandfather, the secondary plot deals with Penitent Brothel's campaign to possess Mistress Harebrain, who is closely guarded by her intensely jealous husband. Ironically, Harebrain is employing, as the spiritual advisor of his wife, Frank Gullman, a courtesan whom Penitent Brothel is employing to seduce Mistress Harebrain. Frank, who is also the mistress of Sir Bounteous, advises the wife how to deceive her husband; and Harebrain is thoroughly hoodwinked.

Follywit cleverly robs his grandfather three times: first, as Lord Owemuch, for whom Sir Bounteous insists on providing his finest hospitality; second, as Frank Gullman; for, to turn his grandfather against her, he rifles the old man's casket and then escapes. Ironically, however, never having before seen Frank, Follywit soon falls in love with her and marries her. Third, he robs under cover of presenting a play at a feast being given by his grandfather.

In the subplot, while Penitent Brothel is with Mistress Harebrain in another room, Frank feigns a godly conversation with her for Harebrain to hear as he waits outside the door. Penitent Brothel has, however, from the beginning, shown a shamed awareness of his own wickedness (I.i.99–105); and, when a succubus in the form of Mistress Harebrain tempts him, he repents. Both he and Mistress Harebrain, becoming fearful, decide to reform. Harebrain is so impressed by their godly talk that he takes Penitent as a friend and invites him to go with him to Sir Bounteous' feast, to which he himself has already been asked.

Follywit and his men disguise as players, whom Sir Bounteous invites to play for his guests. After Follywit has borrowed from the old man a watch, a jewel, and a chain to use as properties in their play, *The Slip,* his accomplices ride away while Follywit talks; but they are soon brought back by a constable. In one of Middleton's funniest scenes, Follywit works the constable into the play, and they bind and gag him before the delighted audience and then escape. Just after the chagrined Sir Bounteous has discovered his gulling, Follywit and his companions enter in their own dress; but, while Follywit is hearing about the robbery, the watch rings in his pocket, and his grandfather discovers all three stolen articles. Follywit then pretends the robbery was a jest, and he assures Sir Bounteous that he is adopting a stable life and has married. Discovering that Follywit has been gulled into marrying the courtesan, Frank, who has been the old man's mistress, Sir Bounteous roars with pleasure over his grandson's mistake, says "this makes amends for all," and gives Follywit a thousand marks.

There is very little integration of the two plots: in Act III, Scene ii, Sir Bounteous visits Frank Gullman; in Act IV, Scene v, Follywit woos the courtesan; and the characters of both plots are brought together physically in Act V at the feast; but the marriage of Follywit to his grandfather's mistress provides the only functional connection of the plots.

Such a comedy contributed to form the concept, in the minds of an older generation, of an amoral or even immoral Middleton. A. W. Ward seemed to think in 1875 that the play was an encouragement to vice; he objected that the rascally hero was not sufficiently punished; and he was not impressed by the "didactic morality" of Penitent Brothel's repentance.[19] One ought to take into account, however, the conventions of "humours" comedy. Follywit's behavior is mitigated by what he calls "the humor of my frolic grandsire" (I. i. 43), which is not to allow Follywit even "poor ten pounds" while the old man lives. Also Follywit's wild, prankish behavior comes more from his love of deviltry and risk than from any criminal or vicious propensity. High spirits condone much. Furthermore, Sir Bounteous tells "Lord Owemuch" that Follywit has "an honest trusty bosom"; and he agrees with his "Lordship" that "that's worth all indeed . . ." (II. i. 131–34).

The courtesan, too, though inclined to be predatory, could be worse; she has never robbed Sir Bounteous though she has had opportunity. She knows all the wiles that women use to deceive, and she imparts them to Mistress Harebrain, who, it seems, is less to blame than is her obsessively suspicious and restrictive husband. At least one can readily understand the wife's natural resentment toward him. Harebrain, another "humours" character, is completely dominated by his sick jealousy like Jonson's Kitely of *Every Man in His Humour*. Penitent Brothel, as his name implies, is construed from the start as capable of repentance; but, though he knows the better, he pursues the worse: ". . . in myself soothe up adulterous motions,/And such an appetite that I know damns me,/Yet willingly embrace it . . ." (I.i.101–5). The dramatic projection of his temptation—appearance of a devil in the form of Mistress Harebrain, who, as he is aware, does not know where he lives—is an impressive means of achieving his reformation. Penitent Brothel's speeches represent the earnest, religious, reforming Middleton of the early poems and *The Phoenix;* and they should be taken seriously.

Allowing for the traditions of comedy and of "humours," which practically never permit presentation of characters in depth, or with many-sidedness, one can say that Middleton created in this play characters that are recognizable individuals with believable motivations. In spite of the hilarious situations sanctioned by the era's dramatic convention, the characters begin to assume greater psychological plausibility than Middleton's earlier ones. However farfetched the situations may be in terms of probability, the play contains abundant references to realistic details of Jacobean life, such as dress, customs, places, and the like. The play has, therefore, both the sprightliness and the realism of the comedy of manners.

It has also an abundance of Middleton's favorite irony. Some of it is directed against Harebrain. The only visitor he allows his wife is Frank Gullman, whom he thinks to be a "pure virgin." He often addressed his wife in a religious strain—for example, "ah, didst thou know/The sweet fruit once, thou'dst never let it go!" She replies: " 'Tis that I strive to get" (I.ii.162–64). The audience has no doubt about what the sweet forbidden fruit is to which she refers.

There are comical ironies too in the household of Sir Bounteous, the primary one being that irony of character that makes him so penurious with his grandson but so eager otherwise to live up to his name. But the most telling irony involves Follywit. When thinking of Frank Gullman, who has acted perfectly the part of the timid virgin, he says: "If e'er I love, or anything move me,/ 'Twill be a woman's simple modesty" (IV.v.70–71). And a moment later: "I ne'er beheld a perfect maid till now." There is also a very special irony in the replies to Follywit of Frank's mother in this scene. Follywit's prologue to the play at Sir Bounteous' feast contains ironical double meanings; but the greatest irony is in the reversal at the moment of discovery that Follywit has married the old man's mistress. Sir Bounteous asks: "Can you gull us, and let a quean gull you?" (V.ii.285). The dénouement hinges, therefore, on the old formula of the biter who is bitten. Indeed, the chief comic idea of the play is expressed in Follywit's foreshadowing remark when he is feeling full satisfaction about his first robbery of his grandfather: "for craft recoils in the end, like an overcharged musket, and maims the very hand that puts fire to't" (III.iii.5–13). "Craft recoils in the end" is the theme of more than one Middleton comedy.

*A Mad World, My Masters* has less sustained satire than *The Phoenix* or *Your Five Gallants;* but, like all Middleton's comedies, it is written in a knowing way, with frequent satirical references (as of a sophisticated urban observer) to the behavior of modern people which reflects the shortcomings of life in the city "nowadays." As in other works of the period, complaint and satire are mingled; such mingling is illustrated by the first dialogue of Frank and her mother (I.i.153–61). The mother comments on the fifteen times she has sold the daughter's virginity; yet there will be plenty of future business: "Th' Italian is not serv'd yet, nor the French: / The British men come for a dozen at once, / They engross all the market . . ." (I. i. 171–73).

Women are viewed satirically in *A Mad World* (II. vi. 30–36; IV. i. 19–24), and the shortcomings of professions are satirized with Middleton's special irony. When the courtesan tells Harebrain that his wife persists in believing "that every sin is damn'd," he replies: "There's a diabolical opinion indeed! then you may think that usury were damned; you're a fine merchant, i'faith! or bribery; you know the law well! or sloth; would some of the clergy heard you, i'faith! or pride; you come at court! or gluttony; you're not worthy to dine at an alderman's table!" (I.ii.131–37). Although some of the satire is ageless, the play also contains a good many satirical references of a topical kind (III.ii.114–19; V.i.30–34).

It is difficult to give an adequate impression of *A Mad World.* Considering it as a whole, one is impressed by the rapidity of the action, the inventiveness behind the complicated intrigues, the wit and satire, the hilarious spirit pervading the main plot. Although these are impressive, the most impressive aspect is the vitality of the characters. Not one is a blank or a lay figure; each is an individual who promotes his own interests. *A Mad World* is certainly one of Middleton's finest comic achievements.

## V Michaelmas Term

*Michaelmas Term* chiefly concerns Richard Easy, a young man from Essex who has just inherited money and is visiting London, and Ephestian Quomodo, a London draper who has been vacationing in Essex, where he found Easy's lands very attractive. Easy is represented, according to his name, as "somewhat / Too open . . . / he is yet fresh, / And wants city powdering" (I.i.57–60). The plot is a classic demonstration, step by step, of the way in which City merchants fleeced trusting young heirs such as Richard Easy.

After the exposition, Quomodo makes plans with his helpers, Shortyard and Falselight, to get the land away from Easy. Shortyard poses as a friend of a friend of Easy's, for whose sake he will help Easy get money if he needs it; in fact, he lends Easy some while the young man is losing at dice; then they soon go to borrow from Quomodo. But Quomodo, alleging that he is unable to lend cash, offers Shortyard (who calls himself Blastfield) a two-hundred pound "commodity" of cloth—supposed to be practically as good as cash. When Blastfield demurs, Easy persuades him to take the cloth. Since there must be a co-signer of the bond—"but for custom sake"—Easy insists on signing. The debt is to be paid in one month. (Quomodo's wife, Thomasine, who watches, is sorry for the young man.) Next, Falselight, as a merchant, offers only sixty pounds for the cloth; and, when Blastfield demurs over selling for so little, Easy urges him into accepting it. In this fashion, Easy ties the noose around his own neck; and, at the end of the month when Blastfield disappears, Easy is arrested for debt. Shortyard and Falselight, disguised as wealthy citizens, give bond for Easy, who binds himself "body, goods, and lands" to obtain his freedom. Meanwhile, Thomasine suffers over his plight; for Quomodo has the young gentleman in his power. Shortyard turns Easy's bond over to Quomodo, and Easy is free. But now Quomodo has possession of Easy's land: he has reached his goal.

The subplot concerns the courtship of Susan, Quomodo's daughter. Her mother favors the suit of Rearage, a gentleman, but father and daughter favor a Scot who calls himself Andrew Lethe, though he is really Andrew Gruel, the son of a tooth-drawer. Londoners see him as "A gentleman of most received parts,/forgetfulness, lust, impudence, and falsehood . . ." (I.i.162–63). His name indicates that he has forgotten his mean past; and he pretends to be so occupied with social matters that he forgets acquaintances overnight. His own mother does not recognize him, and he employs her as a drudge. He also has a pander, who brings him a country wench who is eager to gain finery by any means.

Since Quomodo's triumph over Easy occurs early in Act IV, Middleton has to bring about a reversal against both Quomodo and Lethe in the rest of the play. The draper gets the idea of feigning sickness and death to observe how wife and son will comport themselves after he is gone. As soon as his death is announced, Shortyard rejoices: he intends to deceive Quomodo's son

Sim and take the lands. Thomasine is also glad though pretending grief; and she helps Easy and assures Rearage of Susan's hand. Quomodo, disguised as a beadle, attends his own funeral to hear what people say of him; and he learns that he gained his wealth "by shifts/And cozenages" and that Sim has no respect for him. As a result, Quomodo vows to disinherit his son. When Thomasine marries Easy, she tells him how he was cheated; and, fearing exposure, Shortyard returns documents to Easy. Quomodo signs a receipt, as beadle, for all that is due him—and, to startle Thomasine, he signs his own name. When he discovers that he has signed a release to Easy, he angrily reveals himself; but all insist that he is only a beadle.

Officers take Lethe and his wench into custody, and he is disgraced on what he expected to be his wedding morning. He is exposed as a coward, as a wretch, and as no gentleman. Susan is convinced that he is base: "For now the difference appears too plain/'Twixt a base slave and a true gentleman" (V.ii.12–13). There is the typical Middleton irony in Lethe's plaintive "Have you so little conscience, officers,/You will not take a bribe?" (V.ii.5–6). In a court scene, Middleton assembles all the characters before a judge for exposure and punishment. When it is agreed that Quomodo is either a spirit or a deceiver, he, having to grasp the horns of this dilemma, finally confesses the cozening of Easy. The judge then forces Lethe, revealed as son of Mother Gruel, to marry the country wench; and he banishes Shortyard and Falselight. Since Quomodo has no money left, he evidently cannot pay the "dues of law" (V. iii. 58) that are necessary to be acknowledged as the husband of Thomasine, and she remains Easy's wife.

Middleton takes pains to allot poetic justice at the end of *Michaelmas Term,* and he strongly emphasizes the moral that craft recoils. Shortyard says: "This is the fruit of craft:/Like him that shoots up high, looks for the shaft,/And finds it in his forehead, so does hit/The arrow of our fate; wit destroys wit . . ." (V.i.42–45). The judge tells Quomodo that "deceit is her own foe," and Quomodo develops the idea: "He hits me everywhere; for craft once known/Does teach fools wit, leaves the deceiver none./My deeds have cleft me, cleft me!" (V.iii.75, 94–96).

## VI A Trick to Catch the Old One

*A Trick to Catch the Old One* (1605) has one of Middleton's most efficiently constructed plots. Witgood, the young gentleman hero, is destitute because he has spent all his money on a courtesan, a girl whom he seduced; he has also mortgaged his land to his rapacious uncle, Pecunius Lucre; and he is burdened with debts that threaten his arrest if he goes to London. This dissolute protagonist sees before him nothing but ruin unless he can recover the mortgage and marry a rich London girl. But the good-natured courtesan agrees to help him by posing as a wealthy widow.

It is significant that in the first scene Onesiphorous Hoard comments spitefully on Witgood's situation with the courtesan and informs the audience that his brother Hoard and Witgood's Uncle Lucre are always competing and quarreling. Presently Lucre and Hoard have a violent quarrel; Lucre has bested his rival in a transaction, and Hoard says he will use any opportunity to vex Lucre. One more part of exposition remains: Moneylove and Freedom, Lucre's wife's son, are rivals for the hand of Hoard's niece Joyce, whom Witgood hopes to marry.

Uncle Lucre is so glad that his nephew Witgood has a chance to marry a widow with four hundred pounds a year (who is really the courtesan in disguise) that he is eager to promote the match, particularly to spite Hoard; and he even gives Witgood fifty pounds for clothes, though he is *not* going to give him back the mortgage. Joyce is then freed from her unwelcome suitors: Lucre's wife encourages her son Freedom to woo the "widow" with gifts, and Moneylove tells Hoard that he is giving up his suit to his niece and desires Hoard's good word with the newly arrived "widow." Hoard pumps him, accepts a fee, and immediately deceives him: "Fool, thou hast left thy treasure with a thief,/To trust a widower with a suit in love!/Happy revenge, I hug thee!" (II.ii.42–44). Hoard intends to woo her himself, to get her money, and thereby to confound Lucre and Witgood.

When Witgood's creditors threaten his arrest, he fends them off: if they expect to get their money, they should not mar his hopes with the "widow." Hoping for his "custom hereafter," each creditor advances money for a wardrobe. Meanwhile, the courtesan-"widow" is receiving many gifts: "I am so haunted with suitors, . . . I know not which to despatch first" (III.i.99–101).

Hoard strikes against Witgood by having gentlemen destroy his credit with the "widow," for they tell her the truth about his rioting and his debts. And the courtesan, through a pretended kidnapping, goes off to marry Hoard—having connived with Witgood, who is glad to see her make her fortune.

In this situation, Lucre, blinded by his anger against Hoard and ignorant of the "widow's" marriage, gives the mortgage to Witgood so that he can regain her favor—but Lucre expects him to return it later. Now, however, hearing that Witgood has lost his "widow," the creditors arrest him for debt. Witgood strikes his last blow by alleging a pre-contract between her and himself. She supports him in this allegation, and Hoard is satisfied to pay off the creditors in order to get Witgood to release her from the "contract." The triumphant Hoard, who now wishes to be friends with Witgood and Lucre, invites them to his wedding dinner. Meanwhile, Joyce has been able to direct Witgood how to meet and marry her.

When the characters assemble at Hoard's wedding dinner—which is also a wedding feast for Witgood and Joyce—Hoard's brother and others from the country are shocked to recognize his wife; and they give Hoard the bitter news that he has married Witgood's former strumpet. Her defense against his anger is that she had never told him that she was wealthy. Lucre rejoices that Witgood has worsted his adversary, Hoard makes the best of the situation, and both Witgood and the courtesan vow reformation. Hoard has the final speech: "Who seem most crafty prove ofttimes most fools." Again, Middleton stresses the idea that craft recoils.

The articulation of the plot of *A Trick to Catch the Old One* is extremely smooth. In a sense, the comedy is more realistic than *A Mad World;* for much less disguise is used. The bitterness between Lucre and Hoard is persuasive, and the bond of fellowship in trickery between Witgood and the courtesan is plausibly and pleasantly rendered. The governing idea is the overwhelming attraction of money; so the pursuit of the "widow" is given far more attention than the perfunctory marriage of Witgood and Joyce. The play has fewer witticisms and satirical comments than Middleton's other early comedies, but the situation causes satire to evolve from the action itself. Such satire can come about only when character, as Madeleine Doran says, "is conceived as the motivator of action. The intrigue . . . must be initiated by traits of human nature liable to ridicule and must work itself out to the discomfiture of its initiator."[20] (Thus Hoard and Lucre are ridiculed and discomfited.) Based on mercenary drives, commercial rivalry, hatred, and desire for family advancement, *A Trick to Catch the Old One* is highly characteristic of Middleton's view of the City.

The vilest evils of a usurer's life are stressed in the three Dampit scenes (I.iv, III.iv, IV.v), which, though only slightly integrated into the plot, reveal, "through a sort of dramatic shorthand," the "physical and spiritual destruction"[21] of a usurer. In the first of the three scenes, as Levin has indicated, Dampit, a "trampler," or overbusy, pettifogging attorney, who is now worth ten thousand pounds though he came to London with only ten shillings, tells everyone about his success. But the second Dampit scene exhibits the private reality behind the public front; he is coming home drunk to engage in mutual insults with his servant. The third scene shows the atheistic drunkard Dampit's deathbed, the climax of "a grimly Hogarthian 'Usurer's Progress,'" as Levin says (130). This self-made man who recognizes no obligations, is an "old Harry," a worse and more devilish "old one" than either Hoard or Lucre (134). Thus these scenes of abominable descent and failure contrast with the action in which Witgood rises; and, by contrast with Dampit, Lucre and Hoard are more easily accepted as "ridiculous butts, who represent no moral threat and so can be let off . . . with relatively mild, comic discomfitures" (132).

Not only in the Dampit scenes but throughout the play there is much irony: cupidity constantly creates the ironies that pleased Middleton so much. The liveliest of them come out when Hoard congratulates himself on his wealthy wife; the vision of his new scale of living works on his imagination as he thinks of riding

> to her lands in state and order following; my brother, and other worshipful gentlemen, whose companies I ha' sent down for already, to ride along with us in their goodly decorum beards, their broad velvet cassocks, and chains of gold twice or thrice double; against which time I'll entertain some ten men of mine own into liveries . . . : the sight of which will so vex my adversary Lucre—for we'll pass by his door of purpose, make a little stand for [the] nonce, and have our horses curvet before the window—certainly he will never endure it, but run up and hang himself presently (IV.iv.12–23).

But after these delusory satisfactions of wealth, position, and revenge, the irony is brought home to him when he learns that he has wedded a "Dutch widow."

Though *A Trick To Catch the Old One* has excellent satire which is motivated by the cupidity of the characters, the characters somehow have less vitality than those of *A Mad World.* The plot interest tends to predominate.

## CHAPTER 4

# *Other Comedies*

### I A Chaste Maid in Cheapside

MIDDLETON crowned his career in comedy with *A Chaste Maid in Cheapside* (*ca.* 1613), the climax of his city comedies; for after this play the comedies are of less worth and the tragicomedies and tragedies represent a deepening and darkening of his view of life. Though *A Chaste Maid* shocked Victorian sensibilities,[1] twentieth-century criticism has considered it to be his finest achievement in the genre of city comedy.[2]

This play, like *Michaelmas Term* and *A Trick to Catch the Old One*, has its foundation in the struggle for power so apparent in the Jacobean age, especially the struggle between merchants and gentry. The world of the city is represented by the Yellowhammer family. Yellowhammer is a wealthy goldsmith whose son Tim is at Cambridge and whose daughter Moll will have a dowry of two thousand pounds. The goldsmith, who purports to be a plain citizen still, is writhing with assumed humility and actual pride as he talks of his son: "A poor, plain boy, an university man;/Proceeds next Lent to a bachelor of art" (I.i.150–51). Both father and mother are self-conscious; for they are caught between accustomed proprieties and the new dignities and new possibilities that their wealth has brought and that are symbolized by a daughter who is about to marry a lord and by a son who is eligible for the hand of the lord's "landed niece."

The lord who is to be the Yellowhammers' son-in-law is Sir Walter Whorehound, and around the questions of Sir Walter's marriage and the possession of his lands the whole action of the play and most of the characters revolve. His lands in Wales are bound to pass to a kinsman, Sir Oliver Kix, if Lady Kix should ever have a child; but, after seven years of marriage, she has remained childless. Sir Walter, however, who for ten years has supported a mistress in London—Mrs. Allwit—has fathered seven children. For his pleasure when living in Wales, he has also had a Welsh mistress; but, now that he is marrying Moll Yellowhammer for her dowry, he has decided to present the Welshwoman as his niece and to provide for her by marrying her to Tim Yellowhammer. Sir Walter's servant Davy Dahanna is a poor kinsman who wishes to keep the lord from marrying so that he himself can eventually inherit.

If Moll Yellowhammer's parents persist in bringing about the match with Sir Walter to a marriage contract, Moll will become the traditional victim of enforced marriage. She has no desire to marry Sir Walter, for she has secretly fallen in love with a poor young gentleman named Touchwood, Junior. Her parents know nothing of this secret love that keeps Moll melancholy; and her mother, unsympathetic and critical about her mood, accuses her daughter of being unfit to share a knight's bed. Thus the fortunes of several characters are involved with Sir Walter's marriage: Moll, Tim, and Touchwood, Junior; Davy Dahanna; and Mrs. Allwit and her husband, a satisfied cuckold.

Allwit has been conceived as stingy, base, and lazy; he fervently congratulates himself on having been maintained ("found") for ten years by Sir Walter, to whom he refers as "the founder." All the times of a fat life of ease come to light in Allwit's soliloquy of I.ii.11–56. Sir Walter pays for everything in most generous quantities; but meanwhile, as Allwit remarks, "I have the name, and in his gold I shine." So the gratification of Sir Walter's desires produces the gratification of Allwit's. Many husbands work hard "to buy a paradise for their wives" and are jealous to boot, but Allwit possesses, as he says,

> O, two miraculous blessings! 'tis the knight
> Hath took that labour all out of my hands:
> I may sit still and play; he's jealous for me,
> Watches her steps, sets spies; I live at ease,
> He has both the cost and torment. . . . (I.ii.50–54)[3]

In fact, when Sir Walter appears, he soon shows his jealousy; for he says to Allwit: "Yet, by your leave, I heard you were once offering/To go to bed with her" (I.ii.95–96). He threatens Allwit with marrying and leaving him to support the family if he should presume to approach his own wife. Sir Walter is treated as the master in the Allwit household, and Allwit himself is scorned even by the servants; but the complaisant cuckold is satisfied to loll in ease.

*A Chaste Maid* has a multiple-action plot. The main action concerns the conflict between Touchwood, Junior, and those who oppose his marriage with Moll: her parents and Sir Walter. The second action relates to the fortunes of the Allwits, which are bound up with the decisions of Sir Walter. The third action involves the problem of the Kix family—their childlessness. In addition to these three actions, there is a fourth one, less developed: the courtship and marriage of Tim Yellowhammer and the Welshwoman that Sir Walter has brought to London.

The third action is an important one which brings in Touchwood, Senior, the older brother of Moll's beloved; he and his wife contrast to the situation of the Kixes: "Some only can get riches and no children;/We only can get children and no riches" (II.i.11–12). A loving couple, they have decided to separate because they are producing children too rapidly for the father's capacity to support them. In fact, Touchwood, Senior, is so phenomenally fecund that he says, "For every harvest I shall hinder haymaking;/I had no less than seven lay in last progress . . ." (II.ii.61–62); and a country wench appears bringing his child. He is willing to give her his slim purse, but he advises her to dispose of the baby by some device, which she later does. In contrast, the desperate Kixes constantly accuse each other of responsibility for Lady Kix's barrenness. When they hear that Touchwood, Senior, uses a water for fertility that "never misses," they determine to invest in it, however expensive it may be.

Middleton triumphed as a dramatist by being able to unite all these actions into an artistically integrated play. The play is set in motion by the arrival of Sir Walter Whorehound in London during Lent. Immediately upon his arrival, Mrs. Allwit has another child of his, and Allwit and Sir Walter make arrangements for a fine christening. To avert suspicion, Sir Walter is to be godfather to his own new daughter, a device of which Allwit says he would never have thought. The seducer and "founder" reproves him: "The more slave:/When man turns base, out goes his soul's pure flame,/The fat of ease o'erthrows the eyes of shame" (II.ii.36–38). *Fat* and *ease* are key words in the Allwit situation, and the unctuous hypocrisy of Sir Walter's reproof exemplifies the rich irony so characteristic of Middleton.

The irony is increased by making the Lenten season the setting for self-indulgence.[5] Middleton invents the scene with the promoters (II.ii) and of the christening (III.ii) to show with lively humor and abundant irony how hypocritical, corrupt, and venal English society is. The promoters are informers employed to catch those who are breaking the laws against eating meat during Lent. The satiric exposure of the promoters is climaxed by their encounter with the country wench who brought the baby to Touchwood, Senior. She carries a basket with a loin of mutton exposed and claims to be the servant of a wealthy gentleman whose doctor permits her to eat meat. As she leaves to bring her "master," she has them swear to keep the basket until she comes back. Ironically, they swear, hoping that she will never return—and, indeed, she will not, for beneath the mutton they soon discover her baby.

As godparents of Sir Walter's child, Sir Walter chooses Moll Yellowhammer; and Allwit chooses Touchwood, Junior. Thus the two lovers have opportunity to meet; and Touchwood, Junior, makes plans to slip out with Moll and be married. He has the wedding ring her father made for him, with the posy "Love that's wise/Blinds parents' eyes." On the point of marriage, however, they are discovered by Moll's father and Sir Walter. Pitiless, despite her pleas, Yellowhammer seizes her to lock her away "as carefully as my gold," while Sir Walter takes a high line with the newly met Touchwood, Junior: "one that I must shun like pestilence,/Or the disease of lust" (III.i.51–52).

Meanwhile, Middleton continues his "great naturalistic genre study of the christening celebration." [6] These scenes in which the guests arrive, enter, and later take refreshments are unsurpassed for their satirical rendering of manners and for their portrayal of the sensual indulgence of the visitors (among them two Puritan women) to the obbligato of Allwit's choric comments. Middle-class manners are hit off very effectively: the simpering straining of courtesies by some; the bickering over precedence by others; the iteration by the Puritans of terms like spirit, lowliness, and zeal; the flattered response to the greeting of Sir Walter. Allwit comments on their readiness with food and wine; the comic-satiric strokes fall hardest upon the Puritans. The First Puritan orders: "Bring hither that same cup, nurse; I would fain/Drive away this —hup—antichristian grief" (III.ii.88–89). Later, when Tim Yellowhammer arrives from Cambridge, the First Puritan rises to greet him with "Welcome from the wellspring of discipline,/That waters all the brethren" (III.ii.162–63) and then falls down from the effects of the wine. The pretensions, the greed, and the sensuality of the guests have all been exposed. Behind them, as they depart, they leave a stifling, disordered room and stools wet with spilt wine. The atmosphere is epitomized in Allwit's disgusted remark: "How hot they've made the room with their thick bums" (III.ii.182).

Incited by Davy Dahanna, Allwit attempts to thwart Sir Walter's marriage; but he fails. Then the Touchwood brothers make plans "to strike at this knight's fortunes,/And lay him level with his bankrout merit" (III.ii.9–10). Touchwood, Senior, is willing to help his brother (and gain money for himself) by tricking Sir Oliver Kix with a medication and by secretly getting Lady Kix with child. After a very comic episode Touchwood gets Lord Kix to down his medicine and then to rush off and ride for five hours while his wife takes her treatment "lying."

Meanwhile, Touchwood, Junior, romantically loyal and sure of Moll's heart, has planned to elope that night. He and Moll get to the Thames, but in spite of the friendly watermen's efforts to help them, Moll's mother captures her daughter and drags her home by the hair while both parents abuse the girl; and Yellowhammer decides: "tomorrow morn,/As early as sunrise, we'll have you join'd" (IV.iii.62–63). Such harsh behavior is censured by the watermen: "she cruelly tugg'd her by the hair,/Forc'd her disgracefully, not like a mother" (IV.iii.80–81). Thus Middleton secures sympathy for the romantic young couple and makes more acceptable their determination to resist parental commands.

Sir Walter undertakes to bar the way of Touchwood, Junior, who comes searching for Moll, and the two men draw swords and wound each other. Touchwood, Junior, pursues the knight, but the latter's ardor for sword play has left him; he declares, "I've certain things to think on." In fact, Sir Walter's brush with death has brought about an abrupt change of heart, just as Penitent Brothel in *A Mad World* is shocked into reformation by his experience with the succubus. When conveyed to the Allwits' house, Sir Walter attacks Allwit with such terms as "poison" and "worse than slave or villain"; and he accuses Allwit of having basely connived at his wicked behavior:

> None knew the dear account my soul stood charg'd with
> So well as thou, yet, like hell's flattering angel
> Wouldst never tell me on't, lett'st me go on,
> And join with death in sleep; that if I had not
> Wak'd now by chance, even by a stranger's pity,
> I had everlastingly slept out all hope
> Of grace and mercy. (V.i.26–32)

Allwit does not easily give up; he invites his wife to help Sir Walter regain a better frame of mind. The knight, however, calls Mrs. Allwit a "loathsome strumpet" who has more impudence than the devil and whose weeping makes his situation worse:

> There's nothing but thy appetite in that sorrow,
> Thou weep'st for lust. . . .
>
> . . . this shows like
> The fruitless sorrow of a careless mother,
> That brings her son with dalliance to the gallows,
> And then stands by and weeps to see him suffer.
> (V.i.58–64)

Allwit then has Sir Walter's seven children rushed in to "make him cheerful straight," but Sir Walter sees them as his "vengeance." They darken his hopes of heaven: "Still my adulterous guilt hovers aloft,/And with her black wings beats down all my prayers/Ere they be half-way up" (V.i.75–77). Since the knight refuses to alter or take "comfort," Allwit, who is at his last shift, invites Sir Walter to make his will. Middleton thus has an opportunity to use again the tradition of the mock-testament, as he had in *The Black Book*. Sir Walter bequeaths to Allwit "three times his weight in curses," "all plagues/Of body and mind," and "such a sickness ten days ere his death." He leaves similar bequests to Mrs. Allwit (V.i.97 ff.).

News arrives that Touchwood, Junior, has died of his wound. Immediately Allwit refuses any aid and orders Sir Walter out of the house. He will not even allow him a spare room in the garret. His wife thinks the knight can save himself with a plea of self-defense: "Neither his life nor estate will be touch'd, husband" (V.i.119). "Hear a fool!" Allwit retorts; "his lands will hang him."

The cynical inference is that, since a murderer's lands would be forfeited to the crown, men's eagerness in both Court and City to acquire them must insure Sir Walter's conviction. A final blow comes with a servant's announcement that Lady Kix is pregnant. "All ill at once!" cries the knight.

Some of Middleton's most sardonic irony appears in Allwit's smug, self-righteous rejection of Sir Walter:

> I pray, depart, sirs,
> And take your murderer along with you;
> Good he were apprehended ere he go,
> Has kill'd some honest gentleman; send for officers.
> (V.i.138–41)

With the utmost effrontery Allwit informs the indignant knight:

> I must tell you, sir,
> You have been somewhat bolder in my house
> Than I could well like of; I suffer'd you
> Till it stuck here at my heart; I tell you truly
> I thought y'had been familiar with my wife once.
> (V.i.142–46)

Mrs. Allwit equals her husband's hypocritical show of indignation. Awakened to the vicious reality of their brazen rapacity, Sir Walter cries, "Gamesters, farewell, I've nothing left to play" (V.i.150). A broken gamester, he must leave what he now perceives as a gambling house. The scene ends with a repetition of the image of gambling, as Allwit asserts: "There is no gamester like a politic sinner,/For whoe'er games, the box is sure the winner." Sir Walter was led by lust and desire for pleasure, not by "policy." His generosity has left the Allwits with a magnificently furnished house; they can rent to lodgers and live at ease in a house in the Strand. The politic sinners have achieved a complete triumph over Sir Walter, who, assailed by creditors, is thrown into prison for debt. However great his licentiousness, he is outdone in evil by the smooth-hard Allwits.

The Touchwood brothers have failed in their first two attempts to get Moll away from her parents. In the rest of Act V, Middleton has to present their third, and successful, attempt, as well as additional exposure of the Yellowhammers. Poor Moll is suffering severely from love melancholy, and her parents "spare no cost" to get expensive medicines for her; but she tells them, "Your love comes too late" (V.ii.27). Faithful still to his brother's desires, Touchwood, Senior, brings news of the death of Touchwood, Junior; and he stresses that "the restraint of love, and your unkindness" were worse wounds for the young lover than those from the sword. The crassness of Yellowhammer is revealed in his "now, wife, let's but get the girl/Upon her legs again, and to church roundly with her." Moll swoons on receiving a letter from her lover and is presently borne out dead, in spite of her mother's assurance that "Thou shalt have all the wishes of thy heart/That wealth can purchase!" (V.ii.82–83).

Fearing the severity of public opinion, the parents decide not to appear at Moll's funeral; but the father persists in trying to save something from the wreck of their hopes by marrying Tim to "the rich Brecknock gentlewoman" (V.ii.97). Thus Middleton keeps the Yellowhammers out of the first half of Act V, Scene iv, in which the double funeral of Moll and Touchwood, Junior, is held. As chief mourner, Touchwood, Senior, praises Moll's virtues and asserts that all would rejoice to have seen the couple married. When the company agrees, Moll and Touchwood, Junior, rise up in their coffins;[7] and the parson marries them. After this great theatrical stroke, the Yellowhammers appear, lamenting their discovery that Tim has married Sir Walter's Welsh whore, but willing to acquiesce in Moll's match. The Welshwoman rejoices that marriage will make her honest, and Tim has to make the best of his situation. Middleton ties up the last loose end of the plot by having the grateful Lord Kix offer to support Touchwood, Senior, and his family.

Moll is represented as perfectly virtuous amidst a world filled with depravity, trickery, and corruption. As the pathetic victim of love melancholy and of her parents' cruelty, she has mainly a passive role; but her spirit and her unswerving devotion to Touchwood, Junior, are shown in her willingness to take part in the devious plans for her escape and marriage. Moll's suffering reflects the serious effects of a pervasive mercenary attitude. The comic liveliness with which Middleton has imbued the other parts of the play emerges hand in hand with abundant irony, which, as Schoenbaum says, compensates for a cynicism[8] which does not insist that all the evil characters be punished.

*A Chaste Maid* deserves praise not only for its elegantly structured plot, its exuberant comic action, and its wealth of irony but also for its excellent poetry. The play contains a much larger percentage of verse than do the earlier city comedies. Though Middleton could write sprightly prose, he attained in *A Chaste Maid* a mature poetry that is flexible, natural, managed with great skill, and exactly suited to his dramatic purposes.

## II No Wit, No Help Like a Woman's

*No Wit, No Help Like a Woman's* was not published until 1657, but its composition has recently been assigned to 1612.[9] In the play, a comedy with a relatively complicated double plot, the main plot, apparently of Middleton's invention, concerns the familiar theme of the courtship of a wealthy widow, Lady Goldenfleece. Middleton combined with it a subplot based on an Italian comedy of 1589, *La Sorella,* by Giambattista Della Porta.[10] The Italian source joins Plautine farce with an admixture of serious and sentimental material, but Middleton skillfully condensed the Italian play (so that he could develop his other plot), made it less sentimental, and transferred the setting from Italy to England.

In the Italian play Attilio, the hero, has returned to Nola secretly married to Sofia, a girl from Venice whom he presents to his father as his sister, whom he has ransomed from slavery. Though sent to Constantinople to ransom his sister and his mother, victims of shipwreck and Turkish slavery long before, he fell in love at Venice with a beautiful bondservant; used the ransom money to purchase her freedom; and, never having ventured farther, has come home with the tale that his mother has died. The father decides to marry both his son and his "daughter"—the son to Sulpizia, who is loved by Attilio's best friend, Erotico; and the "daughter" to a braggart captain. Attilio's clever servant Trinca pleases the young men with a scheme to remove Sofia's unwelcome suitor and marry the girl to Erotico while Attilio agrees to the marriage with Sulpizia. The father will supposedly have had his way, but at night each lover can have his desired partner.

Complications develop with the arrival of a letter from Attilio's mother reporting that his sister has disappeared. Trinca tries to trick the father by pretending to translate, from Turkish, the reports of a boy in such a way as to discredit the bearer of the letter; but Trinca fails. When the mother herself comes, Attilio has to tell her the truth; and she not only magnanimously forgives him but also agrees to say that Sofia is her daughter. Unfortunately for Attilio's happiness, it develops that Sofia, his wife, is really the child enslaved along with his mother. For a time, his fears of the horrible sin of incest transform the play from farce to melodrama; but, when it is revealed that Sulpizia and Sofia had been exchanged as babies, a happy ending suitable to comedy is made possible.

In *No Wit,* Middleton preserves the essentials of Della Porta's story. Attilio's equivalent is Philip Twilight, whose father is Sir Oliver Twilight; and they live in London. Philip, having been sent to the Low Countries to ransom his mother and sister, has brought home a wife from Antwerp. She passes as his sister Grace though she is really the daughter of old Mr. Sunset. Philip's mother was not captured by Turks but by "Dunkirkers"; so instead of a Turk as bearer of the mother's letter, Middleton uses a Dutchman. The braggart captain usual to Italian comedy is replaced with Weatherwise, an eccentric "humours" character, who has a considerable part in the other plot as one of the widow's suitors.

In his condensation of *La Sorella,* Middleton eliminated most of Della Porta's rhetoric, but a little of it appears in two scenes: (1) in the quarrel scene (I.i) where Philip's dear friend Sandfield (Erotico) attacks him for disloyalty to their friendship, thinking him a genuine wooer of the supposed Jane Sunset, who is really, of course, Philip's sister and daughter to Sir Oliver; and (2) in the scene (IV.i) where Philip is horrified at the idea that he is guilty of incest. The histrionics in these scenes and in Act II, Scene ii, are in the Beaumont and Fletcher manner. In each scene, however, Philip is restrained and advised by his clever servant, Savourwit (taking the place of Trinca), who speaks throughout in a worldly, dry, and comic style that does much to keep the play from sentimentality.

In the main plot, Mrs. Low-water formulates a plan to recover her husband's lost estate from Lady Goldenfleece, whose uncle by some dishonest means (I.ii.19) got possession of the Low-water property and will not make restitution. Mrs. Low-water (her husband helping her disguised as a servant) disguises herself as a handsome, swashbuckling younger son, for whom the widow (Lady Goldenfleece) jilts her four other suitors. It is Mrs. Low-water's brother Beveril who ransoms Lady Twilight, Philip's mother, from her ten years' imprisonment in the Low Countries, who then brings her home, and who as a scholar is employed to compose a "device" to be presented after the wedding of the widow. As soon as he sees Lady Goldenfleece, Beveril loses his heart to her; and Mrs. Low-water, having refused to go to bed with the new "wife," entices Beveril into Lady Goldenfleece's chamber and then accuses her before the whole company of adultery—an excellent theatrical stroke.

After a great show of outraged virtue by the supposed husband, Lady Goldenfleece finally offers five thousand pounds to induce him to leave. Mrs. Low-water reluctantly agrees to accept the sum, and she also says she could give the widow freedom—on condition that the latter make honest use of it. Lady Goldenfleece begs for freedom; and, when told that her new husband is already married, she chooses Beveril for her mate. After being threatened with death for bigamy, Mrs. Low-water reveals herself as a woman already married—and as the victor in the matter of monetary reparation as well as the contriver of happiness for her brother and the widow.

At this point Sir Oliver Twilight insists on contracting Philip to "Jane Sunset" and his supposed daughter to Sandfield. In order to prevent incest (as she believes), Lady Goldenfleece breaks an oath of secrecy to disclose that the girls were exchanged as babies by their nurse, Mrs. Sunset, who desired her daughter to have wealth and security. With this reversal, the couples are straightened out; and everyone is happy.

As Gordon has pointed out, Middleton invented several connections between his two plots. The characters all know one another; Lady Goldenfleece possesses the secret of the birth of the girls; "Jane" and Mrs. Low-water are relatives; Weatherwise has been the widow's suitor and returns to her when dismissed by Sir Oliver; and Lady Twilight is conducted to England by Beveril, who had ransomed her. Thus the play is reasonably well integrated; and, by using the "thematic framework" announced by the title, Middleton was able to control his "varied material." [11] Two of the women use their wits, and all three give help. Mrs. Low-water tricks Lady Goldenfleece and helps her brother; Lady Twilight tricks her husband regarding her supposed death and the girl, and helps her son; Lady Goldenfleece helps the lovers.

By comparison with *A Chaste Maid in Cheapside* or *Michael-*

*mas Term,* the situations in *No Wit* seem more contrived and less firmly grounded in the conflicts and manners of Jacobean society. Middleton adopted the Fletcherian point of view: to assume a certain unusual situation and then see how the situation might be worked out.[12] Nevertheless, Middleton has infused a good deal of plausibility into his characterizations of Sir Oliver Twilight and Lady Goldenfleece. Sir Oliver's unwillingness to part with his money and allow his daughter a dowry ("I can abide no word that ends in portion." I.i.203), his foibles about keeping all his children in his house, and his indignation at being deceived—these traits fuse into a consistent comic portrait. The widow's responses to courtship, her candid eagerness to marry a virtuous and vigorous young husband, and her honest anger, mortification, and desire for revenge when she has been rejected—all are convincingly realistic; her role constitutes the best of the comedy. Having been told by the new "husband," whom she thought so passionate, that he "can't abide these kissings" and that he will not go to bed with her, she says:

> If I had chose a gentleman for care
> And worldly business, I had ne'er took you;
> I had the offers of enough more fit
> For such employment; I chose you for love,
> Youth, and content of heart, and not for troubles—
> (V.i.34–38)

Then, in a climax of chagrin, shamed by his suspicions of her fidelity and sent to her room to pray, she bitterly deplores her lot:

> Have I yet married poverty, and miss'd love?
> What fortune has my heart! that's all I crav'd,
> And that now lies a-dying; it has took
> A speeding poison, and I'm ignorant how:
> I never knew what beggary was till now. (V.i.777–81)

Mrs. Low-water is also well presented as a resourceful and dynamic person; Middleton gets ironic fun out of the situation of the disguised woman so gallantly courting the widow in the character of a younger brother. However farcical the situation of the courtship may be, the human responses to it are natural and persuasive.

The eccentricities of Weatherwise and the fantastic entertainment he arranges are fairly amusing. For pure fun, however, the best scene is that in which Savourwit tries to discredit a Dutch merchant in Sir Oliver's eyes. The merchant, who has brought the news of Lady Twilight's survival, is going on an errand; and he leaves behind his son, who can speak only Dutch. Savourwit, the servant, pretends to question him in Dutch and then tells Sir Oliver that the boy has informed him that his father talks like a madman at a certain time of the moon and that he could not have seen the girl (Philip's wife) in an Antwerp inn since they had not come through Antwerp. Thus Savourwit, like Trinca in *La Sorella,* misleads Philip's father; he gets Sir Oliver to believe that the Dutchman is trying to swindle him and also was "a little steeped in English beer" (I.iii.190). This is the one scene of his source that Middleton kept in its entirety, and he uses the same sort of climactic joke regarding the characteristics of languages.

For the wedding-entertainment scene in which the disappointed suitors avenge themselves on the widow, Middleton fell back on the contrivance of a "device" prepared by a scholar, a variation of the masque-device by which Fitsgrave exposes the dishonest gallants in *Your Five Gallants.* The playing of the "device" involves much of the spectacular, but Beveril explains that his device is a simple one concerning the four elements, Fire, Air, Water, and Earth—

> This the effect,—that whereas all those four
> Maintain a natural opposition
> And untruc'd war the one against the other,
> To shame their ancient envies, they should see
> How well in two breasts all these do agree.
> (III.i.23–41)

Before the four suitors appear as the elements in Act IV, Scene ii, the stage direction reads: "After loud music for a while, a thing like a globe opens on one side of the stage. . . ." For the idea of the spectacle here Middleton reused part of the *Magnificent Entertainment* that he had written in 1604, the speech of Zeal, who explained that the warring elements had ceased their opposition "at the peaceful presence of their King" (*Works,* VII, 225).[13]

The speeches of the suitors in their show are characteristic of Middleton's early satire. Fire complains: "I was once a name of comfort, warm'd great houses,/When charity was landlord"—but now fire is changed to the fire of avarice, luxury, and the lust of young landlords and of "libidinous widows" (IV.ii.73). Air and Water attack the falsity of widows, and Earth is bitter against Lady Goldenfleece's first husband, whose wealth "he wrung unconscionably from the rights/Of poor men's livings . . ." (IV.ii.166–67). The spectacle is completed when Beveril and three others, all appareled as the four winds, strip the Elements of their disguises so that the widow can give the suitors a scornful requital.

Though *No Wit* has situations, characters, and ideas that are familiar, Middleton handled his material in a lively poetic style. The notable ease of his dialogue resembles that of Fletcher. In addition to the speeches of Savourwit with their wit, word play, and sophisticated imagery suitable to his racy worldliness (I.i.), there is the sprightly boldness of Mrs. Low-water as a younger brother (II), the gentlemanly fluency of Beveril and the suitors (III), and the rousing vigor of the scene where the widow is arraigned for alleged infidelity (V).

In many places Middleton uses imagery that is striking and poetically effective. Sandfield thus accuses Philip:

> I feel thy wrongs at midnight, and the weight
> Of thy close treacheries; thou hast a friendship
> As dangerous as a strumpet's, that will kiss
> Men into poverty, distress, and ruin. . . . (I.i.27–30)

Savourwit remonstrates with Sandfield: "this shows/As if you'd challenge a lame man the field,/And cut off's head, because he has lost his legs . . . (I.i.41–43). During the scene of Philip's first interview with his mother, when the son feels remorse for his conduct towards her, he says, "Now there's no way to 'scape, I'm compassed round;/My shame is like a prisoner set with halberds" (II.ii.79–80). When Lady Twilight agrees to help Philip, she tells him: "You ask devotion like a bashful beggar,/That pure need urges, and not lazy impudence" (II.ii.165–66). Philip, fearing he has committed incest, is told by his mother to repent and pray for pardon; he thus expresses his sense of overwhelming sin:

> O Savourwit, never came sorrow yet
> To mankind like it! I'm so far distress'd,

I've no time left to give my heart attendance,
Too little all to wait upon my soul.
Before this tempest came, how well I stood,
Full in the beams of blessedness and joy!
The memory of man could never say
So black a storm fell in so bright a day. (IV.i.259–66)[14]

Middleton's poetic style, resourceful in pungent and homely realism, is well suited to the comic decorum of the play; and the dialogue drives along with unflagging vigor. Because of these virtues, in addition to its well-articulated and more than adequate characterization, *No Wit* deserves better than the dispraise it has recently received from Schoenbaum and from Barker. Professor Clubb comes nearest the mark with her judgment that *No Wit* is "a funny, well-balanced, and on the whole, better play than *Sorella*. . . . Yet *No Wit*'s superiority is not so much a result of Middleton's improving on Della Porta's material as of his wedding it to a new and amusing subplot."[15] Middleton ably translated *Sorella* from Italy to England, but his invention of the Low-water-Goldenfleece plot entitles him to a considerable measure of praise. *No Wit* is not far below his best comedies in excellence.

## III More Dissemblers Besides Women

In *More Dissemblers Besides Women* (*ca.* 1615) a satirico-romantic comedy set in Italy, the reader has to work his way through a maze of deceptions created by the hypocrisy and scheming of the characters of high rank. Among those of lower rank, one finds some low comedy; the entertainment is mainly from singing and dancing and not much from farce or wit. For the most part, Middleton's style is formal and rather poetic; it lacks the wit and liveliness found in his earlier comedies. But he arrives at his mature style for serious work, that economical, forceful, and precise poetry for which he is admired in *The Mayor of Queenborough* (*ca.* 1618) and *The Changeling* (1622).

In the exposition, Middleton reveals several characters with varying attitudes toward chastity. The Cardinal of Milan, a great champion of chastity, approves of men who have nothing to do with women. His nephew Lactantio has seduced many women and has two mistresses; therefore, in order to remain his uncle's favorite and his heir, he must dissemble. Foremost of the dissemblers in the play, Lactantio hypocritically pretends to scorn womankind and worldly pleasures and to devote himself to divine meditation.

The widowed Duchess of Milan has kept for seven years a vow never to remarry which she made at her husband's deathbed; her virtue and constancy command the Cardinal's supreme admiration. However, since she secludes herself and sees no men, her virtue is never tempted. The first complication of the play arises when the Cardinal arranges to have the Duchess face temptation, for he expects her victory over it to "bring grace to great'st perfection" (I.ii.46). Her first test is to join in welcoming General Andrugio, who is returning victorious. As soon as she beholds him, she falls in love. "I confess I'm mortal," she tells Celia, her waiting-woman. "Is not this flesh? Can you drive heat from fire?/So may you love from this . . ." (I.iii.107–11). She does not know, however, that Andrugio loves Lactantio's mistress Aurelia.

Dissembling with the Cardinal, the Duchess tells him not that she loves Andrugio but that she loves Lactantio. This dissimulation is part of her plan to bring Andrugio to her. Soon the Cardinal, hypocritically abandoning the principles of a lifetime, proposes that Lactantio marry. The young man maintains his dissimulation until the uncle tells him that the Duchess loves him; then he agrees with pretended reluctance to pay court to her. He is really full of joy that his hypocrisy is to gain so great a reward, but he is also full of conceit; he feels that he deserves no less a prize, for "The best dissembler lights on the best woman;/'Twere sin to part us" (III.i.220–21).

Thus Middleton arranges his characters in a circular pattern of pursuit: the Duchess wants Andrugio, who wants Aurelia, who wants Lactantio, who wants the Duchess.

In the all-important confrontation of the Duchess with Andrugio, when she tells him she loves him, she is presented as a noble person who makes the way to marriage with her as smooth as possible for Andrugio. In simple poetic style that befits the occasion, she tells him:

> I never disgrac'd man that sought my favour. . . .
>
> Sir, in as plain truth
> As the old time walk'd in when love was simple
> And knew no art nor guile, I affect you;

My heart has made her choice; I love you, sir,
Above my vow: the frown that met you first
Wore not the livery of anger, sir,
But of deep policy. . . . (IV.ii.183, 186–92)

Carried away by her affection, she allows Andrugio no opportunity to explain his devotion to Aurelia.

Reverses and surprises abound in the final one hundred fifty lines of the play. When Aurelia (who has been disguised as a gipsy) is revealed as a beautiful young noblewoman, the Duchess acknowledges: "she's younger, fairer;/He has not now dishonour'd me in choice . . ." (V.ii.128–29); and she regards her failure as a just punishment for departing from her vow to her dead husband. When Lactantio appears, Aurelia, still dissembling, begs assurance that she may "freely/Enjoy" the man she loves; and the Duchess graciously gives her word. But when Aurelia springs her surprise by announcing her love for Lactantio, he repels her. Driven by a lusty desire for children and determined to get a husband, Aurelia turns back to Andrugio, who manages, out of love, to forgive her.

There is great irony in Lactantio's rebuff by the Duchess. Just after the conceited youth—whom Andrugio had called a "perfum'd parcel of curl'd powder'd hair" (IV.ii.122)—has said, "Where could she make choice here, if I were missing?" (V.ii.176), she turns upon both him and the Cardinal, reiterating her vow; she has decided to give her fortune to religious uses and to enter a convent. Lactantio is obliged to marry his mistress who has just given birth to his child.

Starting with certain premises of situation and character, Middleton has worked the plot to a logical conclusion. He generally assumes, one may say, that every man has his price; nearly all are fallible upon encountering the temptations of passion and, especially, of ambition.[16] Among the characters only Andrugio is thoroughly honest. Lactantio is the worst of dissemblers, but he is never led into self-deception regarding his character or motives. Both the Duchess and the Cardinal are self-deceived: the Duchess misjudges her own disposition, and the Cardinal does not admit to himself how heavily the advancement of his nephew weighs with him. He tells himself that heaven wishes "to reward virtue in him by this fortune" (II.ii.16). Of course, he could not be more ironically wrong.

The title of the play is based in certain proverbial assumptions about women[17] which are glanced at in the Cardinal's reference to "a creature that's so doubtful as a woman" (I.ii.17). The play reveals, however, that men can outdo women in dissembling; the women dissemble because of love, but the men become hypocrites also on account of ambition, and Middleton apparently enjoys the irony of this situation. The characters of the play, driven by desire and self-interest, and blind until the last moment to the truth of their situation, are fallible creatures who victimize themselves. They illustrate Middleton's mature disillusioned and cynical attitude. Thus *More Dissemblers* is rather like Shakespeare's "problem comedies" in tone, and it constitutes a bridge between Middleton's comedies and his tragedies.[18]

## IV The Widow

The title-page of the first edition of *The Widow* (1652) bears the names of Jonson, Fletcher, and Middleton.[19] Whether the play is a product of collaboration or not, it seems likely that Middleton plotted it because, like *Twelfth Night* in relation to Shakespeare's earlier comedies, *The Widow* is a kind of recapitulation of devices used in other Middleton plays. It has a gang of highway robbers, as in *The Phoenix;* a pair of old rivals, as in *A Trick to Catch the Old One;* courtship of a widow, as in *No Wit;* a woman disguised as a man, as in *No Wit* and in *Wit at Several Weapons;* a letter written by a woman but supposed to be by her suitor, as in *More Dissemblers;* and a character frightened into repentance, as are Sir Penitent Brothel in *A Mad World* and Sir Walter Whorehound in *A Chaste Maid.* Also the song at the end of Act III, Scene i (How round the world goes), expresses the idea of the circulation of wealth found in *Your Five Gallants,* and another song at the end of Act IV, Scene ii (Give me fortune, give me health) suggests in its last line an idea stressed in *Wit at Several Weapons:* "He has lands that was born witty."

In the comedy, which has a double plot, the main action concerns the winning of Valeria, the rich widow; and the subplot concerns the attempts of Francisco and Phillippa, Justice Martino's wife, to have an affair. Material that looks as if it might be developed into a third plot, the flight of Martia disguised as a man in order to escape an enforced marriage, and the actions of Latrocinio and his gang of rogues, is finally subsumed in the double plot already established.

As usual, Middleton's plotting is effective, and the parts of the comedy are ingeniously meshed together. *The Widow* is a workmanlike comedy of situation composed in a workmanlike style that is flexible and realistic in the middle-Jacobean manner and that carries the action along with no loss of interest. It has occasional ironies. The irony, however, is not clinching, and the style lacks the poetic power that Middleton's work possesses at its best.

## V Anything for a Quiet Life

*Anything for a Quiet Life* (*ca.* 1620) is a comedy concerning domestic conflict in three households. In the first household, Sir Francis Cressingham is living extravagantly and wasting money on alchemy; and his young wife, who appears to be treating him harshly and selfishly, restrains and reforms him. In the second, Mrs. Water-Camlet, a jealous scold, makes life almost unbearable for her mild husband until she is finally reformed by drastic treatment. In the third, the husband is base and wicked: Knavesby tries to prostitute his wife to Lord Beaufort, but she remains pure and outwits both men. An interwoven subsidiary plot shows the dereliction and subsequent reformation of two young men, George Cressingham and Franklin, Junior. The plot pattern is thoroughly characteristic of Middleton.

Although Sykes, Lucas, and Barker have thought that all the play save the Water-Camlet part is by John Webster, the internal evidence makes it more likely that Dunkel was right in believing the play to be a "typical comedy of London life by Thomas Middleton, but probably revised by John Webster." [20] The handling of the tradespeople; the farcical gullings, which, like Middleton's plays of around 1607, use conny-catching material;[21] and the irony in the later developments of the Knavesbys' situation—all these appear to be typical of Middleton.

The Water-Camlets are a pair of traditional stage characters, a headstrong, violently emotional, jealous and scolding wife and a patient husband. The wife convinces herself that the younger children of Sir Francis Cressingham, whom he has sent to live with the Water-Camlets, are illegitimate children of her husband;

and, threatening divorce, she leaves to stay with the Knavesbys (Knavesby is her cousin). Water-Camlet, who loves his wife, cannot be happy without her; his problem, therefore, is to get her to return, and he offers his apprentice George a new suit if he can succeed in making her come back.

The gulling incidents provide hilarious farce. Very smoothly and naturally the two young men living by their wits make a calculated impression on Water-Camlet and his helpers. Franklin, Junior, poses as a lord with three thousand pounds a year, and George Cressingham as his presumptuous tailor, who insists on his employer's buying cloth-of-tissue worth forty pounds so that his lady may have a new gown she needs to attend a wedding. Then the "tailor" is sent to see whether Sweetball, the barber who is supposed to be the lord's cousin, can lend him one hundred pounds. But George Cressingham, giving Sweetball a little money, has prepared him for circumcising a bashful young patient who has the pox. The young men get away with the cloth, leaving Ralph the apprentice to collect payment from Sweetball. The pedantic barber-surgeon talks soothingly, trying to overcome Ralph's unwillingness to exhibit the source of his trouble; but Sweetball is determined to use his "dismembering instrument" and his "cauterizing iron red-hot." This low comedy of cross-purposes, propelled by numerous *doubles entendres,* is very funny to read and must have been extremely effective in action.

Then Water-Camlet and Sweetball have Franklin, Junior, arrested, but he talks only French and insists that he is a Frenchman who cannot understand their purposes. By pure coincidence Margarita, a French bawd, comes alone and gives him aid. Like the scene of Ralph and the barber, this scene has the virtue of surprise although it is less of a dramatic achievement.

The rejection of Knavesby by his wife (IV.ii) is in Middleton's favorite ironic vein. Knavesby anticipates her return from the lord to whose bed he has ordered her to go: "a good wench, Sib, thou'rt, to obey thy husband. She's come: a hundred mark a-year, how fine and easy it comes into mine arms now!—" Laughing, he asks her to kiss him—"what has dalliance taken from thy lips? 'tis as sweet as e'er 'twas." But she repulses him:

> Never touch me more;
> I'll keep the noble stamp upon my lip. . . .

I have kiss'd
Ambition, and I love it; I loathe the memory
Of every touch my lip hath tasted from thee.
(IV.ii.19–24)

There remain two lively scenes in which George the apprentice wins his new suit by telling the Knavesbys and Mrs. Water-Camlet that Water-Camlet has divorced his wife and is about to marry a French woman. The news brings Mrs. Water-Camlet home frantically jealous to attack Margarita, whom George has induced to come to the shop. Thus the way is prepared for the reconciliation of the mild husband and an eventually chastened wife.

Lucas has remarked on the "wave of exasperation against domineering women" around 1617–20 which is reflected in some plays of about that time.[22] Although *Anything for a Quiet Life* is no better than mediocre, one can credit Middleton with a neatly plotted play with the theme of the authority of the wife or the husband in the home. The attitude evinced is a sensible seventeenth-century one, for the resolution of the comedy reveals that good wives should be traditionally obedient to good husbands but should not obey bad husbands, to whom they may be superior in virtue and intelligence.

## VI A Game at Chess

Middleton's last surviving comedy, *A Game at Chess* (1624), was a triumph of topical satire, but its colors are now considerably faded because of its topicality. It owed its success to the anti-Spanish and anti-Catholic feeling in England that, after raging for several years, reached its height during the session of James I's fourth Parliament, which opened in February, 1624. Middleton composed the play a little later that spring, it was licensed June 12, and it opened at the Globe on August 6 for an unprecedented nine-day run before huge delighted audiences.

The political background of the play requires some discussion. Count Gondomar, the Spanish ambassador, had achieved a notorious ascendancy over King James which English Protestants thought was excessive and dangerous. Gondomar naturally worked for Spanish interests, which it seemed were identical with Catholic interests. He bolstered the tyrannical feelings of James regarding the royal prerogative, and he of course encouraged James in his desire to marry Prince Charles to the Spanish Infanta, Maria. The English were very suspicious of this proposed match. When Gondomar left England in May, 1622, the English people exulted.

In order to increase Spanish good feeling, James relaxed the execution of the laws against the Catholic recusants. Many Catholics in England were released from prison in August, 1622; and preachers who attacked Spain in sermons were imprisoned. Since, at this time, the English were exasperated by reverses in the Palatinate and blamed James for not supporting the Protestant forces there, they were all the more incensed against the Spanish. Indeed, they suspected that the release of the Catholics upon Gondomar's intercession "was likely to be a prelude to a long series of favours to be granted to Spain." [23]

Prince Charles and the Duke of Buckingham started for Spain incognito on February 18, 1623, to negotiate marriage articles in person, win the Infanta, and bear her back to England like some fairy-tale princess. During the seven months that Prince Charles was gone, the English public worried lest he be converted, put to death, or held as a hostage. When Charles finally discovered in August, 1623, that the Spanish were not going to help his brother-in-law Frederick in the Palatinate, the Prince acceded to his father's request that he return. He and Buckingham reached London on the morning of October 6, 1623.

Great exultation was manifested upon the arrival of Prince Charles—safe out of Catholic hands, unconverted to the Catholic faith, and not married to a Catholic princess.[24] Buckingham and the disenchanted Prince now felt distinctly anti-Spanish, along with Parliament and the rest of the Protestants. James still expected Spanish assurances of help in the Palatinate, but in late November the marriage negotiations at last fell through. The Spanish had merely used James's hopes of the match to help keep England from declaring war over the Palatinate. Buckingham, who gave Parliament a biased account of Spanish dealings, led it to petition James to break off negotiations for any treaties with Spain. When Coloma and Inojosa, the Spanish ambassadors, complained, James temporized and the House of Commons and the Lords unanimously voted confidence in Buckingham. The English would brook no more Spanish interference; Parliament was in a mood both for war against Spain and for treating Catholic recusants more harshly. By April, 1624, the only member of the Privy Council who opposed the breach with Spain was Lionel Cranfield, Lord Middlesex; and he was suspected of working with the Spanish ambassador against Buckingham. Buckingham struck back with charges of peculation against Middlesex, who on May 13, 1624, was sentenced to a severe punishment.[25]

During these years of controversy and suspicion prior to the composition of *A Game at Chess,* many anti-Catholic and anti-Spanish pamphlets were published in England, especially in 1622 when James tried to silence the criticisms of Protestant preachers[26] and in 1624 when the public was so warmly stirred by pro-war and anti-Spanish sentiments. Middleton took material for his play from about a dozen such pamphlets, some of them just from the press while he was writing *A Game at Chess.* He made most use of Thomas Scott's *Vox Populi* (1620) and *The Second Part of Vox Populi* (1624), *The Friers Chronicle* (*anon.,* 1622) and Thomas Robinson's *The Anatomie of the English Nunnerie at Lisbon* (1622). He drew to some extent on *The State Mysteries of the Jesuites* (*anon.,* 1623) and on *Newes from Rome: Spalato's Doome* (*anon.,* 1624).[27]

The pamphlet last mentioned relates the unlucky fortunes of Marco Antonio de Dominis, Archbishop of Spalatro, after his return from England to Italy. A learned theologian, he came to feel that the popes had usurped authority, and he wrote his three-volume *De Republica Ecclesiastica* to try to overcome the schisms of the Catholic church occasioned at the time of the Reformation; but he did not dare publish it in Italy. He was encouraged by Sir Henry Wotton's chaplain to come to England, where he arrived in 1616 and was given a very honorable reception by James. He was soon appointed Dean of Windsor and Master of the Savoy; he published his *De Republica* as well as several anti-Catholic pamphlets; and thus he obtained for a time a certain distinction as a convert to the Church of England. His desire for greater preferment, however, which James would not allow him, his worldly ambition and covetousness, led him to embrace the opportunity to recant and go back to Italy after a former friend became Pope as Gregory XV.

Though angry with de Dominis, James finally permitted him to depart in 1622. De Dominis was given honor by the Catholics, however, for only a few months (during which he wrote "an abject repudiation of his anti-papal works");[28] for, when Gregory XV died, the Inquisition condemned de Dominis to prison. After a year of imprisonment, he died. He was then adjudged guilty of heresy, and his body was exhumed and burnt.

De Dominis figures in Middleton's *A Game at Chess* as the Fat Bishop, who is satirized for his ambition and rapacity; but, though a black piece, he is also seen as the victim of Spanish designs—the invitation to return to Rome and destruction being one of Gondomar's many plots. Gondomar is represented in the play as the Black Knight; for, in *A Game at Chess*, Middleton employs conflicting pieces of a set of chessmen. The black pieces represent Spain, the Catholics (especially Jesuits), and evil; the white pieces, England, the Protestants, and good. It seems likely that Middleton chose the game of chess (and not cards, for example) as the basis of his allegory because it was associated with Spaniards, Italians, and the Roman Catholic clergy. Middleton's imagination may have been prompted, too, by the fact that the greatest seventeenth-century chess player, an Italian subject of the king of Spain named Greco, was living in England from 1622 to 1624.[29]

The play, which Boas called "a topical dramatic allegory on Aristophanic lines," [30] allegorizes, from the English point of view, the political relations of England and Spain during the preceding few years, particularly the visit of Prince Charles and Buckingham to Spain. This political allegory, which takes up about 940 lines, is balanced by a more general allegory in the form of a seduction plot, which has about 1150 lines. Various characters in the political allegory can be identified. The Black Knight is, as noted, Gondomar; the Black King, Philip IV of Spain; the Black Duke, Olivares, his chief minister; the Black Bishop, the Father General of the Jesuits; and the Black Queen, apparently the Catholic Church. The White King is James I; the White Duke, the Duke of Buckingham; the White Knight, Prince Charles; the White Queen, the Church of England; the White Bishop, Archbishop Abbot; and the White King's Pawn, the Earl of Middlesex. The characters in the seduction plot do not lend themselves, however, to such identification; for, although the seduction plot exposes the machinations, deceits, and immorality of the Jesuits as represented in anti-Catholic pamphlets, the chess pieces in this plot do not stand for actual individuals.[31]

The play begins with an Induction in which Ignatius Loyola and Error view a vision of the game between the White House and the Black House. Loyola reveals himself as an unscrupulous seeker after power, for Middleton's main purpose in Act I is to impress upon the audience the idea of Spanish plans for universal empire: the Jesuits, both male and female, are "all true labourers in the work/Of th' universal monarchy" (I.i.50–51) at which they aim. In courts and palaces they are busy gathering intelligence which they send to the Father General: "so are designs/Oft-times prevented, and important secrets/Of states discover'd, yet no author found/But they suspected oft that are most sound" (I.i.59–62). The White King's Pawn (Middlesex) gives intelligence to the Black Knight (Gondomar) and vows to help the Blacks. This piece of action prepares the audience for later revelation that the Pawn is wearing black under his white garment. One learns too that the Black Knight honors a Jesuit, the Black Bishop's Pawn, in public though he knows him to be vicious.

The Black Bishop's Pawn in Act II attempts the virtue of the White Queen's Pawn, an innocent devout woman, by trying to convince her that she must show the virtue of complete obedience to her religious advisor. The attempt to seduce the White Queen's Pawn is the one part of the action that runs through the whole play. For a time, the Blacks are in apparent triumph over virtue; but in Act III the White Queen's Pawn is cleared through the efforts of the White Knight and White Duke.

In Act II, Middleton satirizes the Fat Bishop (de Dominis), who congratulates himself that he can live at ease and gormandize in the White House, and who reveals his ambition and his vanity over his books. But the Black Knight is his enemy and has plans to lure him to the Black House and there ruin him. In Act III, the Fat Bishop goes to the Black House after receiving an invitation supposedly from a cardinal. His desire for preferment is satirized: "I am persuaded that this flesh would fill/The biggest chair ecclesiastical" (III.i.9–10); and he admits his worldly materialism: "Ambition's fodder, power and riches, draws me" (III.i.73).

The play is almost broken in two, for the actions started in acts I and II are fulfilled in Act III. Attempts on the virtue of the White Queen's Pawn are renewed, however, in Act III, Scene ii. By means of a "magic glass" the Black Queen's Pawn predicts who the other Pawn's husband will be: none other than the Jesuit who tried to seduce her before, but he is now disguised as a handsome gentleman.[32] The innocent White Queen's Pawn is induced to enter into a precontract to marriage, but her virtue is saved when the Black Queen's Pawn tricks the Jesuit by occupying the marriage bed herself. She turns out to be an Englishwoman who had lost her innocence in a nunnery.

With Act IV comes the beginning of the Black Knight's plan to entice the White Knight to the Black House. The hypocrisy and flattery of the Blacks are revealed with heavy irony in Act IV, Scene iv; and in Act V the White Knight and White Duke are given an elaborate welcome at the Black House. This part of the play is, of course, a portrayal of the visit of Prince Charles and Buckingham to Madrid. Since the visitors had scoffed at their hosts for the poor food they had been served, the niggardliness of the Spaniards is satirized. The Spanish approve their own lack of excess: "surfeit is/A thing that's seldom heard of in these parts" (V.iii.3–4). But their visitors are not expected to live so strictly: they may "eat and eat every day, twice, if you please" (V.iii.67).

Finally, a discussion evolves about the possibility of the conversion of the White nobles. The White Knight doubts that he would be worthy to join the Blacks. He charges himself with the sins of ambition and covetousness, and the White Duke accuses himself of carnality. These sins are approved by their Black hosts. A feast of ambition is provided for the Catholics by the whole of Europe, the main course being "our chief oven, Italy, the bake-meats," with the White Kingdom but "the garden for our cook to pick his salads" (V.iii.89, 85). Covetousness is but "good husbandry. . . . We make the very deathbed buy her comforts . . ." (V.iii.108, 110). As for carnality, it is "the trifle of all vices, the mere innocent . . ." (V.iii.124).

The climax of the discussion, and of the play, comes with the Blacks' treatment of the White Knight's assertion that he is an archdissembler. Dissimulation, says the Black Knight, is the most valuable of qualities, "the only prime state-virtue upon earth" (V.iii.149); if he is a dissembler, he is truly their brother. Upon hearing this statement, the White Knight shouts, "the game's ours; we give thee check-mate by/Discovery, King, the noblest mate of all!" (V.iii.159–60). The Black pieces are pushed "into the bag," and the White House has the victory.[33]

The checkmate "by discovery" involves a pun; the White

Knight and Duke discover the Catholics' policy of dissimulation; and, in the game of chess, checkmate takes place "by discovery" when a piece, for example the knight, is moved and the opposing king is in check from another piece without the second piece's having been moved. Thus the White Knight would check the Black King, and the King would be "discovered" to be also in check from the White Duke (Rook). According to J. R. Moore, such a double check was a method of winning much favored by Greco. The reference to "discovery, noblest mate of all," comes from Saul's *Famous Game of Chesse-Play* (1614): "A Mate by discovery, the worthiest of all." [34]

For all its contemporary success and notoriety, *A Game at Chess* is not one of Middleton's best plays. Though the concept of the chess game makes the play a genuine tour de force, it is loosely plotted and, in places, clogged with source-material that Middleton had imperfectly digested. The best characterizations are the satirical representations of the hypocritical Fat Bishop and Black Knight, but the portrait of the latter falls into the conventional lines of the Machiavellian villain (cf. V.iii.201). Evidently, the pamphlet material is imperfectly digested because Middleton was writing the play with as much speed as possible. Even so, as commentators have indicated, certain passages have great vividness, ironic pungency, or poetic beauty.[35]

## CHAPTER 5

# *Comedies in Collaboration*

MIDDLETON collaborated with Thomas Dekker, William Rowley, and perhaps with John Fletcher, John Ford, and others. His genius for collaboration was best drawn out when he worked with Rowley, not only on a comedy but also on tragicomedies, a masque, and a tragedy.

### I The Roaring Girl

*The Roaring Girl or Moll Cut-Purse* is the result of collaboration between Middleton and Thomas Dekker. The woman known as Moll Cutpurse was the historical character Mary Frith, who was notorious about London for wearing masculine dress, for bearing herself like a man, and for consorting with criminals. She is interpreted in the play, however, according to the romantic predilections of Dekker as an upright, goodhearted girl of great size and strength who, like a questing knight, helps her friends and whose bad reputation is undeserved.

The play was presented about 1608 at the *Fortune* by Prince Henry's Men, but it has much in common with earlier plays by Middleton and by Dekker and John Webster which were written for boys' companies.[1] The original concept of the play was probably Dekker's: it resembles that of the main plot of *The Shoemakers' Holiday,* in which the main point is the removal of obstacles to the marriage of true lovers, the chief obstacle being the opposition of the young man's father. The exhibition of thieves' cant in Act V, Scene i, and the presentation of an unscrupulous old soldier are also characteristic of Dekker.[2]

The double-plot action of the play concerns three groups of characters: (1) Sebastian Wengrave and his father, Sir Alexander; Sebastian's betrothed, Mary Fitzallard, and her father, Sir Guy; (2) friends of the Wengraves, Sir Davy Dapper and his son Jack, plus some other gentlemen; (3) three citizens, Gallipot,

Openwork, and Tiltyard, and their wives, who are being pursued by three gallants, Laxton, Goshawk, and Greenwit. Moll, the Roaring Girl, unifies the play as she moves from one group to another.

The shares of the two authors are nearly even. Dekker set forth the exposition of the main plot in Act I, and Middleton was responsible for the exposition of the subplot of the citizens' wives in Act II, Scene i. Middleton, it seems, wrote Acts II, Scene ii; IV.i; and V.ii; Dekker wrote III.iii; IV.ii; and V.i. The two men collaborated closely in Act III, Scenes i and ii; and it is possible that each man added some touches to scenes by the other.[3]

At the beginning of the play, Sebastian is feigning love for Moll, so that his father will consent to his marriage with Mary Fitzallard. Scorning her small dowry, Sir Alexander vows to disinherit Sebastian if he marries her. The father employs Trapdoor, a bogus old soldier, to try to inveigle Moll into stealing and thus eliminate her. In the subplot, Laxton wishes to make an assignation with Moll at Brainford or Ware;[4] and she makes an appointment with him for Gray's-Inn-Fields, where she is also to meet Trapdoor, who has asked to be hired as her servant. She meets them in man's dress and eloquently takes the part of wronged women against Laxton, whom she wounds after forcing him to fight. She intimidates Trapdoor and reveals him to be a coward, but hires him.

Meanwhile, against the upbraiding of his father, Sebastian maintains that Moll is good; he introduces the idea that she is being condemned "by rote," an idea that re-appears at the end of the play. Moll is willing to help the lovers and, in fact, is true to all her friends. When she visits Sebastian, she of course avoids all the temptations put in her way to steal.

In the subplot Laxton and Mrs. Gallipot play out a farce of a feigned precontract, by means of which he extracts £30 from Gallipot.[5] With Act IV, Scene ii, Dekker takes over the subplot; the city wives expose the gallants who have been bothering them. After Dekker's characteristic manner, all are innocent, and all remain friends. Moll then exposes Trapdoor and Tearcat, who are disguised as poor soldiers needing charity, and exhibits her command of thieves' cant.[6]

In the final scene, Middleton presents the dénouement of the main plot. The climax comes when, thinking that Sebastian has actually married Moll, Sir Alexander finds that he has wedded Mary; and the relieved father gladly returns the son's land to him. Before them all—the two plots are slightly brought together by the presence of the citizens, their wives, and the other gentlemen —Trapdoor confesses his attempts to entrap Moll, Sir Alexander apologizes, and Moll's name is cleared. Sir Alexander declares that he will no longer look with the eyes of the world or "condemn by common voice."

The play is thus largely a vindication of Moll, "the Amazon of the Bankside," as Bullen called her (I,xxxv). The Epilogue promises the appearance on the *Fortune* stage of the historical Moll Cutpurse, but no record indicates whether she ever did appear there. In a Prologue, Middleton writes with disarming modesty of "this published comedy; good to keep you in an afternoon from dice at home in your chambers." The implications of Middleton's remark are reasonably accurate; *The Roaring Girl* is an adequate play for its theater. Though not distinguished, it was constructed by a pair of professionals according to long-established patterns that were mainly romantic and slightly satirical.[7] It represents the first clear example that shows Middleton's genius for collaboration. Its liveliest scenes (III,i,ii) result from close collaboration. In the first, Moll, the chivalrous, confident Amazon, appears at her best as the champion of women. An idealized portrait of a girl of independent and completely fearless spirit who is made on the pattern of generosity and who scorns anything ignoble, Moll is a figure such as Shakespeare's Beatrice in *Much Ado about Nothing* would have been if translated to Jacobean London and to a different social class and if given the necessary physical attributes.

## II Wit at Several Weapons

*Wit at Several Weapons* (1609) was printed in the Beaumont and Fletcher first folio (1647) and was ascribed to them in the Archer play list of 1656. Twentieth-century scholarship, however, has inclined to ascribe the comedy largely to Middleton and William Rowley, without entirely denying the possibility that Fletcher may have had some hand in it.[8] A reader might surmise that Middleton was the author because, first, the names of some of the dramatis personae, especially Sir Perfidious Oldcraft and Sir Ruinous Gentry, are precisely like those of characters in Middleton's undoubted plays. Second, one part of the action concerns a son who tricks his father by means of collusion with a gang very much as Follywit tricks his grandfather in *A Mad World.* Third, closer study shows that versification and diction seem characteristically Middletonian in several scenes; and, fourth, linguistic evidence set forth by Cyrus Hoy indicates a strong probability that Middleton wrote about half of the comedy. It seems reasonable, therefore, to follow Hoy and Barker in ascribing to Middleton I.i; II.i; III; and IV. Professor Hoy believes that Rowley wrote the remainder: I.ii; II.ii-iv; and V.[9]

In the play, which has a double plot, the first one deals with the conflict between Sir Perfidious Oldcraft and his son Wittypate, who is now twenty-one but is refused an allowance by his father until he can prove his ability to live by his wits as his father did when young. Sir Perfidious proudly expatiates on his having thriven by pimping and by taking advantage of executorships of orphans, and concludes:

> I hold my humor firm, if I can see thee thrive by
> Thy wits while I live, I have the most courage
> To trust thee with my Lands when I dye; if not,
> The next best wit I can hear of, carries 'em: . . .
> (I.i. Glover and Waller ed. of
> Beaumont and Fletcher, IX, 68)

The second plot deals with the thwarting of the plans of Sir Perfidious for marrying his niece to a foolish knight, Sir Gregory Fop, who is willing to return to him one-third of the girl's portion. The avaricious but sprightly old man thus serves to unite the two parts of the action.

Sir Gregory brings with him a poor but discreet comrade, Cunningham (whose name is no accident); and Sir Perfidious proposes to play a trick upon his niece by presenting Cunningham as her chosen husband. Cunningham is "to stand for the Anti-mask"; then Sir Gregory will come "forth more unexpectedly/The Mask itself" (I.i, p. 70).[10] With irony characteristic of Middleton, the uncle is thus responsible for making his niece fall in love with Cunningham and for her scorning the graceless Sir Gregory. Cunningham shows his wit, however, by pretending to love the niece's guardianess, an old crone who also has a niece. Though the play has few characters, the arrangement allows varied possibilities for love pairings, jealousy, and intrigue.

In a lively first act, Middleton introduces both parts of the action, that of father and son, involving money and tricks, and that of uncle and niece, involving the gulling of Sir Gregory. In both parts, Sir Perfidious the wit-lover is defeated by a young man who shows a fertile wit. Like Follywit, Wittypate Oldcraft tricks his penurious elder three times; Middleton wrote the part about the second trick, which involves the "robbery of Lady Ruinous Gentry by her husband and other members of the gang. The miseries of Lady Ruinous are well presented at the opening of Act II; poverty-stricken, she finds it painful to hear the word *Lady:* " 'tis a Title[1] That misery mocks us by, and the worlds malice. . . ." As Barker has suggested, the introduction of Lady Ruinous resembles that of the similarly situated Mistress Low-water in *No Wit.* Both characters have the spirit to try to improve the family situation. Lady Ruinous has even helped the gang in robberies. Now she is disguised as a "brave young Gallant" carrying a bag of money.

Wittypate's device is ingenious and rather complicated. In disguise, he has persuaded Credulous Oldcraft, his cousin and his father's favorite, freshly down from the university, to join in robbery. Sir Ruinous poses as a constable who has arrested Credulous and recovered the bag of money. But the "gentleman" robbed insists that the thieves took a diamond, and Sir Perfidious is persuaded to pay one hundred marks, its alleged value, in order to keep Credulous out of court and to save the family reputation. He is incensed, however, with his nephew for such wickedness, and sends him packing. Wittypate has the multiple satisfaction of twitting his cousin about his having "come raw from the University" (IV.i. p. 112) and about his having been cheated; of displanting from favor his "fathers *Cambridge* Jewel, much suspected/To be his heir"; of gaining money; and of outwitting his father. Middleton's invention and irony sparkle in this part of the comedy.

## III The Old Law

Middleton and Rowley based *The Old Law* on one fantastic assumption—that a law is put into effect requiring the deaths of all men when they become eighty years old and of all women when they become sixty. No source for the play has been identified, but the basic situation is a motif widespread in folklore.[11] Supposing such a law were promulgated—the play shows how it would lead in operation to various results—some hilarious, some wry, some horrifying—that bring out many aspects of human greed, lust, and corruption. The play has a great deal of psychological plausibility. Presumably, the appreciation of the psychological effects of such a topsy-turvy-making decree would be chiefly Middleton's.

*The Old Law* is usually dated 1618, although it might have been composed as early as 1614. Portions of the text are from the pen of Philip Massinger, who likely gave it some revision about 1625 or 1626.[12] Middleton probably had the responsibility for the plotting. Rowley wrote the farcical portions dealing with Gnotho, and Middleton the more serious portions about Cleanthes, Hippolita, and Eugenia. So much is generally agreed, but allocation of authorship of the remainder of the play is more difficult. It seems likely that Rowley wrote I; II.i.214–72; III.i; IV.i; and V; and that Middleton wrote II.i.1–213; II.ii; III.ii; and IV.ii. Rowley's characteristic rough verse appears in I.i. Middleton's "Push!" is found at II.i.71, 142. In III.ii, Lysander challenges young courtiers at "weapons"—which are dancing, fencing, and drinking. This contest resembles that of Falso and Tangle with their law-weapons in *Phoenix,* especially the drinking part, in which the last glass is called "long-sword" (cf. *Phoenix,* II.iii.163–66, 238–39).[13]

A representative pattern of possibilities is revealed in the action of the play: (1) Young men with old fathers (Simonides with Creon, other courtiers, Cleanthes with Leonides); (2) young wives with old husbands (Eugenia with Lysander); (3) oldish men with old wives (Gnotho with Agatha); and (4) young men looking for old wives (courtiers and serving men). Except for Cleanthes, those in the first category are eager for their fathers' deaths so that they may inherit property, spend freely, and enjoy pleasure. Their situation reflects the perennial jokes about the impatient young heir. Eugenia, who represents category two, is a wife of nineteen who is married to a man within six months of eighty; her philosophy is to marry an old man for his money—"and then youth/Will make thee sport enough all thy life after" (II.ii.127–28). Those of classification three are eager to eliminate their wives, who are nearing sixty, so that they may marry younger ones; and those of class four are courting widows of fifty-nine so that they may shortly inherit their property.

In Act I, the situation is explained—that Evander, Duke of

Epire, has promulgated such a law—and the effects of the law are shown. How it encourages rapacity and selfishness is stressed very early in the speech of Simonides to the lawyers (I.i.30–41); Sim is eager to send his father, Creon, to execution, but he must be hypocritical with his parents. Cleanthes, who loves his father dearly, is drawn in contrast to the greedy Simonides. Cleanthes assails the cruelty of the decree, the hypocrisy of such sons as Sim, and the eagerness of lawyers to defend the law.

Cleanthes cannot bring himself to acquiesce in the elimination of his father, the eighty-year-old Leonides. He has a plan for the old man to hide himself in a lodge in the forest where the son and daughter-in-law Hippolita will care for him (Hippolita is a worthy mate of Cleanthes, full of pity and tenderness). Though Leonides declares that their plan to save him will be discovered, Cleanthes insists that they can preserve secrecy; for he and Hippolita are one—"Who shall betray us when there is no second?"—and Hippolita assures them that she can be trusted with the secret: "though my sex plead/Weakness and frailty for me" (I.ii.-460–62). So the reluctant, upright father is finally persuaded to try to evade the cruel law through his son's plan.

Other results of the law are brought forth in Act II. While the hypocritical Sim encourages Duke Evander to put Sim's father Creon to death, his mother, Antigona, tries to justify the good judgment of Creon, even though he is aged; his household laws, she says, are "worthy,/Judicious, able, and religious" (II.i.106–7). Against her asseverations, Sim's "I'll help you to a courtier of nineteen, mother," is shocking and, as she declares, unnatural. But the old father is taken away by the Duke's executioner. Cleanthes and Hippolita then appear with a funeral procession, "gaily dressed" and looking joyous. Cleanthes announces the death of his father before the law could take him. Sim then discharges most of his father's servants; he expects to spend too much to be able to keep them.

The next scene shows the young courtiers visiting Eugenia six months before Lysander's birthday, courting her, already calling her widow, and treating Lysander as if he were dead and a ghost. The enraged Lysander curses these "impious blood-hounds" (II.ii.71). When Eugenia sees her cousin Hippolita coming, she dissembles and weeps as if overcome by the thought of losing her husband—"a jewel, cousin;/So quietly he lies by one, so still!"

(II.ii.156–57). Hippolita's pity, goodness, and generosity overcome her desire to keep her great secret; she reveals to Eugenia how they have hidden Cleanthes' father. Eugenia rejoices that she has gained such power over this "easy fool" (II.ii.196).

Lysander then tries to evade the law by acting younger than he is; he takes up dancing, riding, and fencing; and, in a burst of vigor, he even outdoes three of his young rivals. He is not allowed to enjoy his triumph long (nor the audience to sympathize with him), for Cleanthes comes to upbraid his ridiculous conduct. Eugenia praises Cleanthes for his sermon, but he turns on her, denouncing her as a strumpet and as the cause of the old man's destruction. With a vengeful smile, she promises requital: she intends to tell Sim, her choice for her next husband, about Cleanthes' concealment of Leonides.

In Act IV, Scene ii, Cleanthes visits his father. The son is very fearful of discovery: "I cannot be too circumspect, too careful;/ For in these woods lies hid all my life's treasure" (IV.ii.4–5). Both he and his father praise Hippolita for a good woman, but such praise now begins to sound ironical. In what follows, the emotional pitch of the style and the quick succession of turns taken by the plot make the scene typical of tragicomedy; but, because of this scene, the whole play should not be called a tragicomedy. When Evander, Simonides, and other courtiers appear, Cleanthes pretends to be merry. Evander is suspicious; he orders Cleanthes and Hippolita to come there no more and says he will have them watched. Their looks of alarm convince Evander that they are guilty, and he sends Sim and others to capture Leonides. Though Cleanthes tries to assume the guilt of breaking the law, Leonides says he himself is the only guilty one. The executioner takes the old man away, and the others leave.

Cleanthes becomes suspicious that Hippolita has betrayed the secret, but she pretends to be guiltless and falsely suspected. "What shall I say to all my sorrows then,/That look for satisfaction?" asks Cleanthes (IV.ii.219–20). Eugenia appears, laughing and letting Cleanthes know she has taken revenge. When Cleanthes thinks to take poison, the miserable Hippolita confesses: "Her tears that never wept, and mine own pity/E'en cozened me together, and stole from me/The secret, which fierce death should not have purchas'd" (IV.ii.241–43). Retribution should ensue, Cleanthes decides: "all we are false ones,/And ought to suffer. . . . We are all tainted some way, but thou worst,/And for thy infectious spots ought to die first" (IV.ii.245–51)—and he starts toward Eugenia.

The seriousness with which Middleton developed the action goes briefly beyond the bounds of comedy, although the cowardice of Sim, who reappears with the courtiers, brings the play back toward the comic. But the author deepens Eugenia's sensualism with one more grotesque stroke; she urges Sim to court her by attacking Cleanthes, who declares: "Thy thirst of blood proclaims thee now a strumpet." She reveals her cruel depravity by her reply: " 'Tis dainty, next to procreation fitting;/I'd either be destroying men or getting" (IV.ii.265–66). The guard then arrest Cleanthes.

Rowley created in Gnotho a memorable clown-figure, who in the farcical scenes reveals how members of the lower classes respond to the opportunities provided by the law. He bribes the parish clerk to falsify the record of his wife's birth so that his poor Agatha will seem on the verge of sixty instead of fifty-nine. There is excellent low comedy in his logic chopping, her attacks upon him, his attempts to get her eliminated, and her efforts to evade the law and death. Finally Gnotho and the serving-men of the low-comedy plot join in a funeral and bridal procession, taking Agatha to the executioner and the bride-to-be to the church.

As usual, all the characters are gradually assembled in Act V. Lysander and Cleanthes are brought to trial before the young courtiers as judges, whose character is shown by their agreeing before the trial to condemn Cleanthes. During the proceedings he has a chance to assail them for unnaturalness, inhumanity, and parricide and for turning everything into disorder. Evander appears, removes the young judges from power, and, with a stunning reversal, has all the old men enter—all are still alive. Cleanthes and Hippolita are made the censors of young men and young women, respectively, in Epire.

After the serious matters have been settled in the court, the characters of the subplot enter for a hilarious close: Gnotho, fiddlers, and all the members of the funeral-bridal procession (the technique resembles that in Shakespeare's *Merchant of Venice,* the gay foolery of Act V following the trial scene). With some difficulty, Gnotho is forced to understand that the law has been repealed and that he and his disgruntled companions must take back their old wives.

The comedy ends with a tribute to law—which might remind one of *Phoenix*. In fact, other aspects of the play resemble *Phoenix:* Cleanthes is a resolute good man who wishes to right wrong, like Fidelio and Phoenix, though he does not have power to do so; Evander, the Duke, like the Duke in Shakespeare's *Measure for Measure,* has been making trial of his people, and he can reward and punish, like Phoenix.

Middleton's best contributions to *The Old Law* are the characterizations of Hippolita and Eugenia, women whose natures he took particular interest in analyzing; the play exhibits again his knowledge of feminine psychology. And it is an excellent example of Middleton's version of Jacobean realistic comedy in which greed for money and for carnal pleasure dominates nearly all the characters. Their selfishness and hypocrisy are plainly revealed as triumphing, once the restraints of tradition and respectability are removed. Essentially, the play is an exemplum to demonstrate the importance for society of traditions codified into laws which protect the "prerogative of age" and allow no opportunity that "the rude son should strike his father dead." [14] *The Old Law* is an epitome of conservatism.

# CHAPTER 6

# *Tragicomedies*

As the Jacobean era developed, Middleton accommodated himself to its increasingly romantic tastes and had a hand in three tragicomedies. The first was the poor and tasteless apprentice work, *The Witch*. Then he collaborated with Rowley on one of his finest plays, *A Fair Quarrel*, and, finally, though most of the writing was done by Rowley and Ford, he adapted from Spanish sources the musical-comedy-like entertainment, *The Spanish Gipsy*.

## I The Witch

While reading Machiavelli's *Florentine History*, Middleton decided to use a story regarding Alboin, King of the Lombards, as the basis of a play.[1] Alboin overcame King Commodus, married his daughter Rosmunda, and "mov'd by the barbarousness of his nature, he caus'd a Cup to be made of her Father's Skull, and in memory of that Victory, drank out of it very often." Having conquered northern Italy, he held a victory feast at Verona, "where much drinking having exalted his spirits, and *Commodus* his Skull being full of wine, he caus'd it to be presented to Rosmunda the Queen, . . . declaring (and that so loud she could not but hear) that at a time of such hearty and extraordinary Mirth, it was fit that she should drink one cup with her Father." The Queen, who resolved to have revenge for the insult, used for her purpose Almachilde, a young Lombard who was striving to seduce one of her maids. The maid pretended to favor him, and one night he was brought to a very dark place where Rosmunda took the place of the maid. Then Rosmunda, revealing herself, presented him with a choice: "whether he would kill *Alboino*, and injoy her and her Kingdom, or be kill'd himself for vitiating his Wife." Almachilde choose to kill the King, but he could not gain the kingdom after the murder because the Lombards were loyal to the memory of Alboin. Therefore, Almachilde and Rosmunda, "packing up with all the Jewels and Treasure they could make, . . . marched off to *Longinus* at *Revenna* [*sic*], who receiv'd them honourably." [2]

Middleton turned this source material, basically shocking for its barbarism, bloody ambition, and implacable revenge, into the tragicomedy of Fletcherian pattern, *The Witch* (*ca.* 1614). In Middleton's play, Sebastian, a young noble, has returned from three years at the wars just in time to attend the marriage feast of Isabella, to whom he had been betrothed ("She is my wife by contract before heaven/And all the angels, sir" [I.i.3–4]); but she has suddenly been married to one Antonio by order of her uncle, the Lord Governor of Ravenna. Thus, the victory celebration of the original story is changed to a marriage feast during which the Duke spitefully requires the Duchess to drink from her father's skull. She vows vengeance through her husband's death.

Since the historical episode takes up less than a paragraph in Machiavelli, Middleton needed to expand his plot material greatly. So he used not only the romance of Sebastian and Isabella[3] but also the affair of Antonio and his whore Florida; the arrangement for secret childbirth by Francisca, Antonio's sister, on the part of Aberzanes, her seducer; the plans of the Duchess to do away with Almachildes and marry the Lord Governor to secure her power; and the repairing to Hecate the witch for magical help by Sebastian, Almachildes, and the Duchess.

Middleton also transfers the whole action from the Germanic barbarousness of the sixth century to the dissoluteness of the Jacobean age. As the play opens, riot and surfeiting are emphasized; and Antonio, the bridegroom, is still going to maintain Florida after his marriage. Running through the play is an element of lubricity. After the pledging from the skull-cup when the newly married couple are retiring, the Duke tells them, according to the old formula, "A boy tonight at least; I charge you look to't,/Or I'll renounce you for industrious subjects" (I.i.146–47). Ironically, however, Antonio and Isabella are unable to consummate their marriage because Sebastian has obtained charmed snake skins from Hecate; and the power of the charm is such that "neither the man begets nor woman breeds,/No, nor performs the least desires of wedlock . . ." (I.ii.158–59). Thus Isabella is kept chaste though she speaks like a married woman to a maiden when she addresses her sister-in-law Francisca. Francisca, already pregnant, is a sensual, heartless girl, whose lewd ironies match the callous self-indulgence of her lover Aberzanes. Middleton also stresses the itchy sexuality of the witches.

Evidently, he has his characters consult witches in order to capitalize on the interest of the audience in witchcraft, and the material about it he gleaned from the chief Elizabethan source, Reginald Scot's *Discovery of Witchcraft,* plus a few lines from Ovid.[4]

Middleton introduces spectacular and musical devices into *The Witch.* The witches sing a song, "Come away, come away" (III.iii.39 ff.), and Hecate sings "A Charm-Song," "Black spirits and white" (V.ii.60 ff.). Since stage directions in *Macbeth* refer to these songs, it seems likely that the King's Men "enhanced" *Macbeth,* when audiences had come to expect this kind of material, by having Middleton write in a part for Hecate and by introducing these songs and some dancing. Though the songs and dances fit *The Witch,* they are completely incongruous in the Shakespearean tragedy.[5]

*The Witch* is developed by intrigue. Middleton makes it fit the formula of tragicomedy by means of the schemes and counter-schemes of the Duchess, Almachildes, Sebastian, Antonio, Florida, and Francisca. All-important and most plausible in the pattern of the play are the responses of the honorable Isabella and the totally selfish Francisca, who foreshadows Eugenia in *The Old Law.* Plot mostly rules, however, as the blindness and mistaken purposes of the characters lead to constant unexpected turns in the action. Finally, with irresponsibility excessive even for tragicomedy, everything is made right for a happy ending.

Not until the eighteenth century was *The Witch* published. It was printed from a manuscript, the title-page of which says that the play was "long since acted by His Ma$^{ties}$ Seruants at the Black-Friers." The play would be dated, then, after 1609, and probably in 1614. Judging by the author's dedication to Thomas Holmes, *The Witch* was a failure; for Middleton calls it "this ignorantly ill-fated labour of mine." Presented by the best company in London for the highly sophisticated audience of the *Blackfriars,* it presumably failed for reasons inherent in the text; but whether it was too complicated, too silly, or too irresponsible one cannot tell. It probably represents Middleton's first effort at tragicomedy, and the modern reader is likely to regard it only as an example of misapplied ingenuity.

## II A Fair Quarrel

*A Fair Quarrel*, published in 1617 *As it was Acted before the King*, springs from the concern over dueling and its increase, which received much attention in the second decade of King James's reign. Before James was crowned, dueling had been a problem, and the arguments against it had been set forth; but, partly in emulation of the French, both English and Scots were becoming almost as "curious in the preseruation of their honour" [6] as were the French nobles. King James's hatred of dueling became exacerbated in 1613, and he told Sir Francis Bacon, attorney-general, to prosecute in the court of the Star Chamber those who tried to arrange, or to fight, duels. Bacon did bring into the Star Chamber a pair who had carried a challenge, and they were imprisoned and fined heavily. Bacon published his *Charge* to the court; the court "gaue warning to all young noble-men and gentlemen that they should not expect the like connyuance or tolleration as formerly . . ."; and the king himself issued *A Proclamation against private Challenges and Combats* (February 4, 1614).[7]

Thus dueling was one of the hot issues of the times. The king and the courts insisted that it was completely without legal sanction, had no justification in terms of trial by combat, and could not even be called honorable.[8] Evidently, however, this official view did not agree with that of many persons, especially soldiers, who were hypersensitive regarding their honor. Though John Norden agreed with other moralists[9] about the foolishness of duels and the necessity of Christian virtue, patience, and self-control, he also understood the contemporary soldier's attitude: "But when a man's reputation is touched by slaunder or disgrace, there seemeth such an honest quarrell, as may not (in credite) be qualified, without the combat, or denial: for so deare doth a souldier seeme to prise his honor, that if it be impayred by any of his companions, he standeth upon his reputation to maintain it with the force of his own sword." [10]*A Fair Quarrel* does not support the official view that a duel is never justified; it presents a test case in which a most scrupulous hero is affronted by a most contumelious opponent. The play should have furnished intense interest for its audiences of 1615–17.[11]

*A Fair Quarrel,* on which Middleton had the collaboration of William Rowley, is a considerably better tragicomedy than *The Witch.* Tripartite in its thematic structure, the play is worked out on three levels, each representing a different scale of values, a different attitude toward life: the heroic, the romantic, and the farcical. The characters of the main plot, who have an aristocratic attitude, accept with utmost seriousness the heroic virtues of honor, justice, and magnanimity; and they see their very souls at stake according to their conduct. The second level is that of the middle class, in whom mercenary attitudes prevail, whereas romantic love struggles against them for the welfare of virtuous hearts. The third level is that of fools and pretenders; among them, insulting rodomontade, boisterous exercise, and other physical satisfactions hold first place and prevent the recognition of the significance of either love or honor.[12]

One is tempted to assume that a play so complex in design was planned by Middleton. There is general agreement that he wrote those parts in which the main plot (the first level) is carried forward, the scenes involving Lady Ager, her son the captain, his friend the colonel, and their duel (II.i; III.i, iii; IV.ii, iii). A second plot (the second level) concerns the love of Jane Russell and Fitzallen and its attempted thwarting by her father. A third action (the third level—a semiplot dependent on the second plot) brings in a suitor favored by Russell for his daughter, the ridiculous Cornishman Master Chough, and his man Trimtram. In Act I, the first two plots are introduced; and all three are resolved in Act V. As Barker indicates, evidence of style and versification makes it likely that, saving possibly some twenty-five to forty lines at the beginning of the play, Rowley wrote acts I, V, and II.ii; III.ii; IV.i and iv.[13]

The exposition of the play is efficiently set forth. The mercenary values of Russell are established immediately, for he says that he had "liv'd on the freeborn portion of his wit," (I.i.5), a remark indicating his business enterprise;[14] but, now that he is wealthy, he insists that (out of tender care for his daughter) he must marry her to riches. He is scornful of Fitzallen, his daughter's beloved; the father has found out all about Fitzallen's debts, and he has a plan to disgrace him before the girl. Thus, Russell is identified as a harsh, mercenary father; he is presently called "a rich churl" (I.i.139).

Next the intense love of Lady Ager (Russell's sister) for her son the captain is made clear. He has just returned from war abroad, and since he is her only surviving child, the mother's devotion to him is doubly strong (I.i.32, 35). The characterization of the captain and the colonel soon begins through the argument of their two friends. The captain's friend adduces that Captain Ager, though young, shows true nobility and not weakness in having "an anger more inclin'd to courage/And moderation than the Colonel"; the captain is a man of conscience who must know whether "the cause be good" before he will fight (I.i.44–47). From words, the two friends immediately go to swords in a a foolish fight which demonstrates the common lack of forbearance and the truth of King James's conviction about "the slaughters . . . strangely multiplied and encreased in these later times . . ."; for men's judgments that "in other things shew gravitie and moderation" are "strangely bewitched, and as it were enchanted in this kinde with the very dregges of *Circe's* Cup. . . ." [15] Russell's comment on their fighting constitutes an ironic criticism of such hotheaded behavior; but his attributing the cause to wenching, contrasts his bourgeois scheme of values with that of a higher social class: "Here's noble youths! belike some wench has cross'd 'em,/And now they know not what to do with their blood" (I.i.52–53).

Soon the captain and colonel arrive, and the colonel is incensed that he should be measured with other men; but Captain Ager finds such an attitude improper to friendship (I.i.74–76). The captain shows little tact; the colonel quickly loses patience, feeling that he has suffered an insult to his valor; and the two men draw swords. Russell succeeds in calming them somewhat, and the colonel's friend warns him against spoiling Fitzallen's hopes of winning Russell's daughter. Being Fitzallen's kinsman, the colonel accedes. Russell then insists upon having all their swords, so that there will be no breach of the peace in his house; but he actually does so to prevent their helping Fitzallen when he has that young man arrested.

When Russell's dissembling is revealed, the colonel is right to be indignant with the "blood-sucking churl" (I.i.341), as he calls Russell. The circumstances and their own natures now push the officers inexorably into a deadly quarrel. Ager feels that he has to defend his uncle. "Pox on your uncle . . . !" cries the colonel. "You are a foul-mouth'd fellow!" cries the captain. Then the colonel shows how foul-mouthed he can be: "thou'rt the son of a whore!" (I.i.348–51). The deadly insult has been passed, both clamor for their swords, but Russell keeps the weapons. His putting the weapons away serves the double purpose of furthering his disgrace of Fitzallen and of postponing the duel. Rowley and Middleton develop this scene with utmost skill to insure that the man of conscience, Captain Ager, will be the injured party and that the duel will be inevitable.[16]

Middleton follows the excellent opening by an even finer scene. The captain's soliloquy (II.i.34) emphasizes further the matter of his conscience.[17] He is exceedingly scrupulous, desiring literally to be certain that he has a *true* basis for undertaking the duel (or quarrel). He will not act without knowing that his cause is just. He reminds himself of woman's proverbial frailty: "She's but woman,/Whose frailty let in death to all mankind" (II.i.28–29); yet he feels shame at the idea of affronting his mother with the question of her chastity. He informs her of the insult to her honor but as if the colonel had defended her against someone else. Middleton gives him eloquent poetry in lines 80–83, and the mother speaks fine dramatic lines in her indignant rejoinder.

Overjoyed by his mother's defense of her reputation, and impatient to fight, Captain Ager tells her the truth; and she is dismayed. In her panic over possibly losing him, she decides abruptly on the course she must take; then she hesitates, tries to stop him merely by her maternal authority, and finally plunges into her hastily constructed lie: "I was betray'd to a most sinful hour . . ." (II.i.185). Having made her anguish and her action completely convincing, Middleton does not deal with her much more in this scene. In the face of the blame with which her son assails her, she creeps out in shame. Shame is now his portion too; he feels "dark and dead to all respects of manhood" (II.i.206) and cut off from honorable men: "I am not for the fellowship of honour" (215). Indeed, his refusing to fight and his determination to exonerate the colonel appall his friends. He is guilty of "blasphemy/To sacred valour!" (250).

In the rest of Act II, Rowley advances the subplots;[18] but Middleton picks up the main plot again in Act III, Scene i. Captain

Ager and his friends arrive at the dueling ground. The First Friend states very plainly Ager's situation: his whole life's reputation and his whole future are at stake. The captain's way of dealing with the matter—his mildness in the guise of Christian ideals—seems to the rest mere caviling, the product of cowardice. Ager's attempt to have the colonel express repentance is inevitably regarded as an additional insult:[19] "I sorry? by fame's honour, I am wrong'd!/Do you seek for peace, and draw the quarrel larger?" (III.i.99–100). But, when the colonel calls the captain "Base submissive coward" (112), the captain changes: "Now I have a cause" (114). Captain Ager feels certain that he has never been a coward. All are surprised that the captain should fight now after refusing combat on account of the slur upon his birth. They fight, and the colonel falls. The captain's statement, "Truth never fails her servant, sir, nor leaves him/With the day's shame upon him" (III.i.167–68), reflects the old idea behind the trial by combat, that God gives victory to him whose cause is just.[20] The colonel too acknowledges that he deserved to lose: "O just heaven has found me . . ." (III.i.176 and ff.); and he repents. He praises Captain Ager—"most valiant and most wrong'd of men" (III.i.184)—and hopes for his forgiveness.

According to the conventions of tragicomedy, the colonel's sudden change is not implausible. Also the colonel is governed by strict conventions; since the captain has taken the conventional means of showing that he is a man of honor and not a coward, the colonel can behave as a gentleman toward him. The colonel's behavior also resembles that of other Middleton characters whose brush with death or with the supernatural leads them toward reformation: Penitent Brothel, Sir Walter Whorehound, and Francisco in *The Widow*.

In Act IV, Scene ii the colonel tells his sister that he has left her his whole estate provided she will marry Captain Ager. Since she hates Ager for injuring her brother, she becomes angry. The colonel is intent, however, upon making noble and magnanimous restitution to the man whom he injured by his ferocious anger. For his peace of mind and salvation of soul, she agrees to do as he asks.

In a very short scene (III.iii) Lady Ager, still worrying over her son, reveals that she lied to preserve him. The purpose of this scene is to inform the audience of the truth so as to prepare for Act IV, Scene iii, in which the son confronts his mother. It also produces an emotional effect through the mother's remorse, sorrow, and fear. When he comes home, Captain Ager is saddened by the thought of his mother's falsity. Lady Ager, jubilant at seeing her son alive, manages between her joy and her upbraiding of him for risking his life, to tell him how she lied in an attempt to preserve him. He kneels to her in joy, for he can now fight the colonel in an honorable quarrel. She sees the irony in her situation: " 'Tis ever my desire to intend well,/But have no fortunate way in't" (IV.iii.84–85). Her sacrifice of good name, she feels, deserves better than a second risking of her son's life. Her sorrow prevails upon the captain not to challenge the colonel. When the colonel's sister comes to offer herself to the captain with the colonel's estate, her beauty instantly prevails with Ager. He rises to the height of the colonel's magnanimity as he raises her up, saying "with that reverence I receive the gift/As it was sent me" (IV.iii.120–21).

Both Lady Ager and Russell because of their concern for their children place "an inferior good above the real value at stake" in each plot: safety over honor and money over love. Their misdirected solicitude leads them into acts that complicate the plots: the lie of Lady Ager and the arrest of Fitzallen. The plots begin together in Act I but do not meet again until Act V. The Chough semiplot is also involved in the dénouement. The dénouement brings the complete reconciliation of the captain and the colonel, who has been raised to the noble level of the captain, and the reunion of Jane Russell and Fitzallen after Russell's supposed cleverness has failed to win him for son-in-law a "rich simplicity of great estate" (II.ii.195), as he calls Chough.[21]

To some extent, *A Fair Quarrel* reflects the city atmosphere of Middleton's early comedies, to which Middleton has added the new Beaumont and Fletcher heroics. The action takes place in London, not in some exotic setting. The tragicomedy of Beaumont and Fletcher commonly impales characters on dilemmas from which they can escape only by ingenious, surprising, and frequently unlikely devices. Middleton and Rowley are to be commended for composing in *A Fair Quarrel* a tragicomedy with a complicated plot structure that is excellently controlled; with an appropriate dash of the Beaumont and Fletcher heroics in a situation involving conflict of honor and a higher principle;[22] and yet with remarkable psychological penetration.

## III The Spanish Gipsy

*The Spanish Gipsy* was licensed for acting by the Master of the Revels on July 9, 1623; but it was not published until 1653, when the authorship was assigned to Middleton and William Rowley. The play was first acted, and was probably composed, while Prince Charles and the Duke of Buckingham were in Spain; they had left England on February 18, 1623. The consequent topical interest of the play perhaps occasioned a need for haste in preparing it, and the necessity of haste may have caused Middleton and Rowley to ask another writer for his help. H. J. Oliver believes that "in 1621 and the next few years, Ford was beginning to collaborate, probably at their invitation, with professional playwrights like Dekker and Middleton. . . . His assistance would probably be called for most often when a play of topical interest . . . had to be written rapidly. . . ."[23] The political situation and the interest of the British public in Spain during the early summer of 1623 enhance the possibility that John Ford was invited to collaborate on *The Spanish Gipsy.*

No one suspected the presence of Ford's hand until 1924 when H. Dugdale Sykes attributed most, if not all, of the play to Ford. R. H. Barker agreed with him, and M. Joan Sargeaunt thought Ford responsible for the Roderigo-Clara plot but not for the Gypsy scenes. Critics have found it difficult to make precise allocation of parts of the play to different authors; and the difficulty is the greater because, as Boas wrote, *The Spanish Gipsy* is a "conventional type of romantic comedy." Oliphant said that it "seems in the main to be from the workshop of Ford and Dekker."[24] If Dekker's name had been attached to it, one would be hard put to it to prove that Dekker had no hand in its composition.

The most significant evidence for Ford's contribution is the presence in certain scenes of the play of *d'ee* and *t'ee* for *do you* and *to you.* (These forms are concealed in Bullen's edition of Middleton and in most editions by normalizing them to *d'ye.* Such normalizing is the reason the student of the older drama must always consult original editions.) Ford habitually used these Devonshire provincialisms, as well as *girl* pronounced as two syllables. There is thus strong reason to think that Ford contributed to scenes in which these provincialisms appear.

Sykes was certainly wrong, however, in ascribing the authorship of the play "substantially, if not wholly," to Ford. There is strong evidence that Rowley wrote the parts in which the Gypsy subplot is presented, and perhaps more. Sancho and Soto resemble the foolish suitors in Rowley's *A New Wonder*,[25] and also the suitors disguised as fools in *The Changeling*. Weak, superficial, and frequently coarse puns characteristic of Rowley are also found in the subplot. Sancho and Soto first appear at II.i.117, and Rowley's puns are soon in evidence: "jack" (123) and "purging comfits"—"loose" (125–26). Presumably all of II.i is by Rowley. Sancho and Soto reappear in II.ii during lines 120–79, an interval of boisterousness, superficial wit, and weak puns: "maps"-mops (150–53), and "I have an uncle in Seville, I'll go see him; an aunt in Siena in Italy, I['ll] go see her" (154–5). The Gypsies appear in Act III, Scene i and Act III, Scene ii, where Soto's rough, four-beat couplets (59–72) seem very Rowley-like. The Gypsy plot predominates in Act IV, most of which is probably by Rowley. On the basis of the Chough-Trimtram part of *A Fair Quarrel*, it would seem that Rowley wrote the play within the play in IV.iii. The Gypsies also have a share in V.i and V.iii, parts of which are probably from Rowley's pen.

Ford's "d'ee" shows up at III.iii.40: "My Lord, d'ee know this Crucifix?" In this scene, probably all by Ford, Clara finds herself once more in the chamber where she was ravished. One would expect the scene to be by the same hand as I.iii, in which Clara pleads with Roderigo in that same chamber. Then Act I, Scene iii is likely by Ford (though "Pish!" favored by Middleton comes at line 13). Ford's "d'ee" and "t'ee" also appear in both the early part of V.i—"Why pray d'ee mock my sorrows?" (44); "So, so, I come for Justice "t'ee" (76)—and the early part of V.iii: "What d'ee mean granam?" (24); "But why d'ee use mee thus?" (26); and "I may be bold/To make a suite t'ee" (54–55).

Certain lines in V.i show resemblance, however, to Rowley's style. Line 121 is a nine-syllable line, with a syllable missing after the caesura: "Is not more white: will you pity him?" Lines 126 and 131 are nine-syllable lines: "She has almost melted me to tears" and "by a base Villaines hand, it madds me" (Quarto). Line 200 is either a light line or a line with a missing syllable after the caesura: "In Spain 'a lives; more, not far from Madrill." All these lines are characteristic of Rowley. In V.i.104–12, Constanza accuses Louis of being too young to make a good judge and draws a contrast between young judges and old ones. This suggests the passage in *The Old Law* where Hippolita calls into question the capacities of young men to make good judges (V.i.49ff.), a passage presumably by Rowley.[26] It seems probable that V.i.83–208 of *The Spanish Gipsy* is by Rowley. It seems probable, also, that Rowley brought the play to its end by writing V.iii.65–110. There is a little roughness in the verse (65–70) and an air of jollity that seem more characteristic of his writing than of Ford's or Middleton's.

The following allocations of authorship may, therefore, rather safely be made: Ford: I.iii; III.iii; V.i.1–82; V.iii.1–64; Rowley: II.i.; II.ii.120–79; III.i, ii, in part; IV.i, in part; IV.ii; IV.iii, in part; V.i.83–208; V.iii.65–110. As for what remains for Middleton, Barker asserts: "I think I can safely say that the play never reads like Middleton." [27]

But it is possible that Middleton shared in the authorship. If he did, it may reasonably be assumed that he did the plotting and was the supervisor of the composition. Oliver (29) observed that I.i is too slight for reliable attribution and that I.ii shows no evidence for attribution to Ford. There is nothing against Middleton's authorship of these scenes, and it would be reasonable for him to write the beginning of the play. In Scene i, Roderigo uses *ha'*, and at lines 50–51 there occurs "these villains/Have robb'd us of our comfort. . . ." Both *ha'* and *comfort* are characteristic of Middleton's usage. Oliver also thinks II.ii is not by Ford, but II.ii.1–119—which has to do with Clara-Louis and Louis-Alvarez —does not seem like Rowley's work, and line 109, which reads that "Her loss was usury more than I covet," is not uncharacteristic of Middleton; and *covet* is a word he uses rather frequently. Oliver suggests (p. 30) that Roderigo's soliloquy of III.i.1–30 may be by Ford, and so it may; but there is nothing in it that strongly suggests his writing or that seems impossible to Middleton.

If we assume that the songs of *More Dissemblers Besides Women* (especially the Gypsy song, IV.i.88–113) are by Middleton, it seems likely that he composed the songs of *The Spanish Gipsy* in III.i.111–42 and III.ii.83–112. The chorus of the latter sounds like the Hecate-lines of *The Witch*. Also the song with references to flowers (IV.i.65–80) is comparable to that in Middleton's Entertainment Number 8.[28] Middleton may also have written V.ii, the scene in which forgiveness averts the duel between Louis and Alvarez. It fits with the attitude of magnanimity expressed in *A Fair Quarrel.*

One other parallel with Middleton's work may be noted. At IV.i.175–76, Juanna Cardochia proposes to John. He replies: "'Las! pretty soul./Better stars guide you!" In *The Widow* Villetta proposes to Ricardo. He replies: "'Las, poor soul! where didst thou love me first, prithee?" (IV.i.135). Middleton, then, may have been responsible for I.i, ii; II.i.1–119; III.i.1–30; V.ii; and for the songs in III.i, ii and IV.i. In his capacity as supervisor, he would have gone over the play, smoothing out inconsistencies and giving it a final polish.

This romantic tragicomedy had its source in the *Novelas Ejemplares* of Cervantes. Material from *La Gitanilla* (*The Little Gipsy Girl*) was combined with material from *La Fuerza de la Sangre* (*The Force of Blood*).[29] Possibly the success of Jonson's masque *The Gypsies Metamorphos'd* in the summer of 1621 influenced the choice of Gypsies as subject;[30] but Middleton had earlier used them with much the same spirit in *More Dissemblers.* The title, *The Spanish Gipsy,* emphasized both Spain and Gypsies though the Gypsy plot is distinctly subordinate to the Roderigo-Clara material.

The Roderigo-Clara plot is based on *The Force of Blood,* Cervantes' story about Leocadia, the beautiful daughter of an old hidalgo, who is abducted and ravished by a young Spanish nobleman. His victim, locked in a dark room, gets a window open and is able to observe the furnishings of the chamber by means of moonlight. In her sleeve, she conceals a crucifix, which she retains after being released blindfolded.[31] Rodolfo, her ravisher, soon journeys to Italy, where he remains several years; and the young woman bears a son, who greatly resembles his father. After some years, the boy is injured by a horse and taken for treatment into the house of Rodolfo's parents. He stays there during his convalescence, being visited by his mother, who recognizes the room in which she was raped. Rodolfo's parents perceive the great likeness of their little patient to their son, and they are easily persuaded of the truth of Leocadia's story, which is corroborated by the crucifix. They command Rodolfo to come home to be married; but, when he arrives, they show him the picture of an ugly woman, who, they say, is to be his bride. He refuses to marry except for beauty. Greatly smitten with the loveliness of Leocadia, his partner at a dinner, he is overjoyed to discover that she is the woman really intended as his bride. Thus, honor is restored.

The Constanza-John plot is based on *The Little Gipsy Girl.* Cervantes' Gypsy girl, the beautiful and unusually wise Pretiosa, is loved by Don Juan, a noble young Spaniard, who joins the Gypsies for two years; during this time Pretiosa will be able to satisfy herself whether he will make a suitable husband. Don Juan, who takes the name of Andrew as a Gypsy, is tormented by jealousy; and, because of it, he kills a man and is in danger of being executed. Pretiosa's Gypsy grandmother Guiamara then tells the corregidor of the city that Pretiosa is really his daughter, stolen as a child by Gypsies, and that Andrew is really a nobleman. The story is based on the old motif of the maid supposedly of low degree who turns out to be of high birth.

*The Spanish Gipsy* follows its sources closely in many respects, even to small details. One suspects that its authors saw in the sources possibilities for two strongly contrasting love stories. In the first story, as it was adapted, the initial brutality of the lover (Rodolfo-Roderigo—who emphasizes his noble rank) is succeeded by true love and repentance; the ravished lady (Leocadia-Clara) must become willing to marry her ravisher. In the second, the girl (Pretiosa-Constanza) establishes all the requirements; and the lover (Don Juan-John), renouncing the privileges of his rank, acquiesces in her demands. The jealousy of Cervantes' original is ignored so that the sweetness and idealism of love can be stressed.

In order to join these two plots, the authors of *The Spanish Gipsy* create two characters, Alvarez and Louis. Louis is developed from one of Rodolfo's anonymous companions in the original. He is enamored of Clara, fearful that Roderigo has harmed her (Roderigo lies to him, letting him think the girl was returned unharmed), and, at the end, angry with Roderigo for having won her away from him. Louis' father has been killed by Alvarez in a duel twelve years previously, and Louis desires revenge. Alvarez was banished; however, though people think he is in Rhodes, he has secretly returned. He and other aristocrats disguise themselves as Gypsies. His wife is the sister of Don Fernando, corregidor of Madrid. She had charge of Don Fernando's daughter, Constanza. There is no question of the daughter's having been stolen by Gypsies; she is presumed to be dead. Thus, Louis is binder in the plot as the lover of Clara, the enemy of Alvarez, and the friend of Diego, who is wounded by John. Alvarez binds the plot by being the leader of "Gypsies," the husband of the corregidor's sister, and the object of Louis' revenge. The efficient dramatic adaptation of the material is characteristic of Middleton and resembles that of *Women Beware Women.*

A few other adaptations of the Cervantes sources were made. The page-poet lover of Pretiosa, Don Clemente, becomes Sancho, an English clown type, who is given a man, Soto. This pair, who fit Rowley's interests and abilities, furnish rather boisterous vaudevillian comedy. A play within the play is used for showing to Roderigo the picture of an ugly woman who is supposed to become his wife. After Roderigo (as the Prodigal Son) is shown treating his (play) father defiantly, he is reproached by his real father, who then requires him to marry the ugly heiress to save the family fortunes. Roderigo refuses; he longs to marry the beauty he has seen in the audience of the play; and his father consents to the marriage if he can win her. She is, of course, Clara, the lady he had wronged, who has desired either marriage or revenge.

A happy ending is made possible in the other plots by a reconciliation between Alvarez and Louis. Alvarez reveals himself in order to make Louis (eager for punishment of John, who had wounded Louis's friend Diego) secure a reprieve for John. At the dueling-ground, Louis is so impressed by the courage and repentance of Alvarez that he forgives him: "I am o'ercome;/Your nobleness hath conquer'd me . . ." (V.ii.45–46). The situation here resembles that of *A Fair Quarrel.* Though Louis challenges Roderigo for having won Clara (Roderigo had seemed a scrupulous friend by announcing his departure for Salamanca), Louis apparently forgets about the matter. Thus the Alvarez-Louis feud is used to unite the actions of the play, and the potentially tragic material is made to conform to a comedy ending.[32] The happy ending is brought about for the Roderigo-Clara plot in V.i, for the Louis-Alvarez plot in V.ii, and for the John-Pretiosa plot in V.iii.

The play fits the Beaumont and Fletcher type of tragicomedy; suspense is maintained to the end, the necessary information being withheld until Guiamara's revelation insures the felicity of both John and Pretiosa.[33]

# CHAPTER 7

# *Pageants, Masques, and Miscellaneous Writings*

PROMINENT among Middleton's "dramatic by-forms" [1] are the seven Lord Mayors' shows that he produced during the period from 1613 to 1626. These shows, patterned by the expectations for such festivities, are squarely in the emblematic tradition so vigorous in the Jacobean age. As Jonson used the masque to try to instruct the court, so Middleton, through his shows, could remind the populace and the members of the city administration of the virtues ideally to be maintained [2] and teach an appreciation of the honor conferred upon each mayor as he joined the long roll of magistrates stretching back to Sir Henry Fitz-Alwin in 1209 or possibly 1189.[3]

The lord mayor of London is always a member of one of the city companies. The pageant for the mayor's installation each October 29, "on the morrow next after Simon and Jude's day," complimented allegorically the mayor and his company; praised London and, frequently, the commerce that made the city rich and powerful; and encouraged the new magistrate to act according to the highest traditions of his office. The members of the mayor's company contributed the money for the civic festivity, and work on it was begun some months in advance.[4] The writer plotted the whole action and composed the speeches, and a craftsman constructed the physical part, the pageants and chariots with their arches, globes, animal figures, and the like. Middleton's partner in these undertakings was usually Garret Christmas, a skilled designer.

These shows, or triumphs, had a pattern of presentation that varied little. Attended by dignitaries, the mayor went from Guildhall to the Thames and thence by barge, "in company of his worthy Brethren and attended by all other Companies in their seuerall Bardges made fit for triumph,"[5] to Westminster, where he was presented to the barons of the Exchequer. On his return, he left the river at Baynard's Castle and proceeded to several points, where parts of the show were exhibited: St. Paul's Churchyard, the little conduit in Cheap, and St. Lawrence Lane. After a dinner in Guildhall, the procession attended a religious service in St. Paul's, and the mayor finally reached his home by torchlight and was treated to a last spectacle and speech.

The shows were elaborate and costly. In 1617 the Company of Grocers paid Middleton, as writer and producer, £282 for his *Triumphs of Honour and Industry.* But the total expenses were £882, 18*s*, 11*d*. They included money for 124 gowns; 124 javelins; 24 dozen white staves for whifflers, marshals, and porters; 49 dozen large torches; shot, powder, and six score chambers; 32 trumpeters, 8 drums, 4 fifes, and the city waits; and 50 sugar loaves, 36 pounds of nutmegs, 24 pounds of dates, and 114 pounds of ginger, "which were throwen about the streets by those which sate on the griffyns and camells. . . ."[6]

## I *Lord Mayors' Shows*

For *The Triumphs of Truth* (1613), Middleton's most elaborate show, he worked up a "germinal idea"[7] from Jonson's courtly masque *Hymenai* of 1606. Jonson has a conflict of Truth and Opinion; Middleton of Truth and Error; in both works Truth triumphs over several vices; but Middleton's show acts out things only described by Jonson.[8] Middleton may also have taken a suggestion or two from Dekker's *Troia Nova Triumphans,* the pageant of 1612, in particular the conflict of Virtue and Envy; but Middleton's Envy is the champion of Error.

In the show itself, soon after the departure of Sir Thomas Middleton of the Grocers' Company from Guildhall, his reverend mother, London, addresses him to remind him that she has reared him and "set wholesome and religious laws before/The footsteps of thy youth" (Bullen, VII, 237). She encourages him to proceed "in ways of goodness; glory is best won/When merit brings it home." (238) At the Thames, the procession discovers five islands with "Indian fruit-trees, drugs, spiceries, and the like; the middle island with a fair castle especially beautified"—evidently in honor of the recently formed East India Company's success in establishing a factory at Surat in 1612.[9]

At Baynard's Castle, the Mayor is received by Truth's angel on horseback and Zeal, the champion of Truth, "his right hand holding a flaming scourge, intimating thereby that as he is the manifester of Truth, he is likewise the chastiser of Ignorance and Error" (239–40). The angel warns the Mayor of the mists of Error, but she and Zeal encourage him to go on. They conduct him to Paul's Chain, where Error waits to assault him. Error's champion, Envy, rides before, "eating of a human heart, mounted on a rhinoceros, attired in red silk, suitable to the bloodiness of her manners! her left pap bare, where a snake fastens; her arms half naked; holding in her right hand a dart tincted in blood" (241). The emblematic nature of the pageant material is very evident in such a description.[10]

Error the tempter says down with Virtue, "And let thy will and appetite sway thy sword" (242) while sergeants Gluttony and Sloth serve the Mayor, and take bribes for "measure and light bread"—"Make use of time then, thou'st but one poor year. . . ." Zeal forces retirement of "these hell-hounds" and makes way for the chariot of Truth, "in a close garment of white satin, which makes her appear thin and naked, figuring thereby her simplicity and nearness of heart to those that embrace her. . . ." Zeal then interprets the symbolism of Truth's costume (the pageant writers take pains to see that no message is lost) and reminds the Mayor that he came to his present eminence by following the ways of Truth. The significance of English trade with Morocco (begun in 1551) is glanced at by showing a king and queen of the Moors.[11] Then Time, father of Truth, with hourglass, wings, and scythe,[12] orders the procession on to Cheapside to see additional struggles of Truth against Error. Finally, at the Mayor's own gate, after a sermon by Truth, her champion Zeal shoots a flame from his head to destroy the chariot of Error; and Middleton closes with the customary acknowledgments to his coworkers. The action reminds one of morality play traditions. Indeed, Withington was tempted to call this show a "peripatetic morality-play." [13]

Though Middleton won a competition with Munday and Dekker for the contract to produce the 1617 show,[14] his pageant, *The Triumphs of Honour and Industry,* was much briefer than his show of 1613. Since it was again prepared for the Grocers, he had Indian youths working "in an Island of growing spices," and India sitting on a rich chariot between Traffic or Merchandise and Industry. Industry emphasizes the fame to be achieved through work: "Fame waits their age whom Industry their youth" (Bullen, VII, 298–99). But merit is necessary.

Middleton praised *The Triumphs of Love and Antiquity* (1619) as a masterpiece of Garret Christmas' workmanship and his own invention. He took pains to praise Sir William Cockaine not only as magistrate but as military commander. For the Skinners' Company, Middleton provided "a Wilderness . . . with divers kinds of beasts bearing fur. . . ; the presenter the musical Orpheus . . . ; over his head an artificial cock [Cockaine's coat of arms], often made to crow and flutter with his wings" (318). The wilderness thickets represent the political vices of the city. The title indicates the strong pressure of history in this pageant. The Mayor must make himself worthy of the former mayors who were Skinners and of the twenty-one Plantagenets who were free of the Company (admitted to privileges of membership).

The show of 1621, *The Sun in Aries,* suggests that the sun is entering "the spring-time of right and justice" (339). This show seems more commonplace than some of Middleton's pageants; in fact, he tends to repeat himself in the shows that follow; but these pageants left little scope for originality. He begins his account of *The Triumphs of Honour and Virtue* (1622) in the same way as the show of 1619; and his Queen of Merchandise, "a black personage" representing India, parallels the king of the Moors in *The Triumphs of Truth. The Triumphs of Integrity* (1623) again stresses attainment of honor by those who sprang from humble beginnings. Middleton complimented King James with a closing spectacle on the eight Beatitudes. The king's motto, *Beati pacifici,* received special emphasis.

Middleton's last pageant, *The Triumphs of Health and Prosperity* (1626), begins and ends with a rainbow to indicate London's rejoicing after the plague of 1625, when no show had been given. Sir Francis Drake was commemorated with a Golden Fleece on the top arch of a Sanctuary of Prosperity. Drake was "England's true Jason" [15] (406); and as the magistrate "takes a year's voyage," he must "sail, then, by the compass of a virtuous name." (407) This show was very short, there were complaints of poor performance, and apparently Middleton and Christmas were not paid in full.[16] Though Middleton's early shows were certainly better than the stodgy mediocrities of Munday, and though he seems to have set forth city views faithfully enough, one may surmise that he became bored with the triumphs. He stretched a few ideas a long way over the whole series, which after 1621 became more and more mechanical.

## II *Masques and Entertainments*

Middleton's *Inner-Temple Masque, or Masque of Heroes* was performed between January 6 and February 2, 1619.[17] Probably it owes something to Jonson's imitation of the Mummers' Play, *Christmas His Masque*, of 1616.[18] As Jonson's masque has ten sons and daughters of Christmas—such as Mis-Rule, Post and Paire, and Wassall—Middleton speaks of relatives of Kersmas, who are various games of cards and boisterous Christmas games; and he presents various days of the New Year. But Middleton introduces, for variation, the old mock-testament motif that he had used in *The Black Book* and in *A Chaste Maid.* When Dr. Almanac comes from the funeral of the Old Year, Plumporridge (a fat clown part acted by William Rowley) brings the last will and testament of Kersmas, which Dr. Almanac reads: a list of satirical bequests. The New Year enters and finally allows Fasting-Day to come on Candlemas Eve, whereupon Time proffers his service to New Year.

Middleton uses two antimasques. In the first, Dr. Almanac gives their charge to a "dissolute rout" of days: Shrove-Tuesday to pull down bawdyhouses and attack playhouses (as apprentices did on Shrove Tuesdays)[19]; Ill May-Day, to be an unruly rascal; Midsummer Eve, to get drunk. New Year objects that the charges have been given "at the wrong end," but Dr. Almanac says that "To bid 'em sin's the way to make 'em mend,/For what they are forbid they run to headlong" (ll. 191–92). The second antimasque, with eight boys, involves three Good Days, three Bad Days, and two Indifferent Days, according to their designation by Thomas Bretnor, an almanac maker. Middleton satirizes the way people heed the motto that Bretnor gives for certain days: "A punctual lady will not paint, forsooth,/Upon his critical days, 'twill not hold well" (ll. 208/9).

After the second antimasque, Harmony appears with her "sacred quire," and two songs are sung prophesying good things for the New Year—fruitfulness, glory, and virtue, which is represented by nine heroes, the masquers themselves sitting in nine arches of clouds. After they have danced twice, Harmony sings a third song, inviting them to choose their ladies—as they do, and then dance with them. Finally, Time "closes all." Although the last part of the masque resembles the Lord Mayors' Shows, Middleton, to entertain the members of the Inner Temple and their ladies, made his work quite topical and used a fair amount of satire. The masque should have been reasonably effective.

Middleton collaborated with Rowley on another masque, *The World Tost at Tennis,* originally "intended for a royal night" (Prol., line 12), but it was apparently refused for court entertainment at Denmark House and was presented sometime in late spring or summer, 1620, by the Prince's Men. It has a connection with Middleton's civic activities at this time, being dedicated to Charles Howard Lord Effingham and his wife, the daughter of Sir William Cockaine, whose wedding occurred on April 22, 1620. Middleton's "Epistle Dedicatorie" declares that the work is still not untimely, for their joys will last forever.

The authors concede in the Prologue that their "Courtly Masque" is not usual fare for the public theater: "This our device we do not call a play, . . . /There's one hour's words, the rest in songs and dances" (ll. 1, 13). It is obvious that Rowley wrote the first half and Middleton the second (after the entrance of the Starches). Rowley's part is mainly a commentary on the ill state of the times for the soldier and the scholar. When Time weeps over the dominance of greed and evil living, Jupiter explains that the world enjoyed an age of happiness before Deceit and Pride ruined it. Among other evils, Pride caused "the frenzy of apparel, that's run mad" (367); and this reference to clothing introduces the five Starches, who come dancing to a "light fantastic air." They quarrel for precedence, dance, and leave. Jupiter calls them daughters of Deceit, which "has vex'd the world/From age to age,/And tost it from his first and simple state/To the foul centre where it now abides" (409–11). This is the theme of the masque, how the world (a literal "orb") is tossed from Simplicity to a King to a Land-Captain to a Sea-Captain to a Flamen to a Lawyer to Sovereignty and back to the King—each of them refusing to pass it to Deceit. Song and dance are interspersed, and the show naturally includes compliments to the King.

*The World Tost* is a peculiar hybrid; it has more masque elements than usual with a play and more poetry than usual with a masque; but it is filled with the allegory characteristic of masques and pageants.

Middleton's *Honorable Entertainments,* which survive in a unique copy of 1621, are emblematic representations; created for mayors or civic occasions, they mingle praise, encouragement, and civic pride with morals expressed through little sermons. These ten pieces (to which "An Invention" [Bullen, VII, 369–78] should be added) may have helped their author, as Bald suggests, to win the office of City Chronologer; and some of them—to use Bald's phrase—"attain a rather rudimentary dramatic form." [20] Most of them were composed for Mayors' feasts. In the last two, Middleton created a kind of spring pageant with Flora as chief character and with some rather agreeable verse and singing about flowers. Most of the material in the *Entertainments* is indistinguishable from that of the Lord Mayors' shows.

## III *Miscellaneous Writings*

In 1609 Sir Robert Sherley, who had been in Persia for eleven years, was sent by the Shah as his ambassador to Poland. Sherley's agent, a Master Moore, evidently furnished Middleton with information which he included in a pamphlet, *Sir Robert Sherley Sent Ambassadour. . . ,* an artificial, labored, and incoherent encomium to Sherley's qualities and reputation. It may have earned Middleton a bit from Sir Thomas Sherley, Jr., to whom the second issue is dedicated.[21]

Though the pamphlet *The Peace-Maker* was once ascribed to King James,[22] both internal and external evidence shows that it is by Middleton.[23] In the *Calendar of State Papers, Domestic,* there is recorded a license to William Alley on July 19, 1618, "at the nomination of Thomas Middleton, for the sole printing and publication of a book by Middleton called 'The Peace-Maker, or Great Britain's Blessing.'" King James himself signed the license, and he had told Secretary of State Naunton to "draw up a license that might make the publication a profitable one for Middleton." [24] The king did not assert authorship of the pamphlet. Lacking time to write as much himself as he wished, he sponsored much writing and rewarded authors as he could.[25]

*The Peace-Maker* is written in a mannered, highly rhetorical, euphuistic style. Much of it is patterned stylistically on sermons of the day, and it is filled with flattery of James and with exaggerated praise of peace achieved in England. After a rhapsodic introduction, many paragraphs of which close with *Beati pacifici* (Blessed are the peacemakers, the motto of James), Middleton's discussion is divided into four sections; each is introduced by a rhyming couplet; and each is imagined much like one of the "triumphs" in a pageant. The first, for example, after "*Detraction snarls, and tempts fair Peace to show,/The plenty of her fruits. . . ,*" gives the criticism of Detraction and the reply of Peace. The second shows Peace against those, like beasts or hounds, who molest her—various sins and then Envy, Revenge, and Murder. The third is on the attitude of wise men who do not easily become stirred to dueling on account of a foolish regard for reputation. In this section Middleton inserts (without acknowledgment) some passages from Bacon's *Charge*.[26] Middleton asserts that the man who kills, even in the name of Honor, breaks divine Unity, which sustains all things. The fourth section is introduced by: "*Peace enters here in arms and overthrows/By force of her own strength her strongest foes*"—which are War and the challenger or duelist, the "base imitator" of War.

The pamphlet sermon has a biblical framework. England is like Israel; King James, like Solomon: "Here sits Salomon, and hither come the tribes for judgment" (Bullen, VIII, 327). Though the King could take this passage as a tribute to his wisdom, Middleton probably had in mind the verse "and he had peace round him on euery side" (I Kings, 4:24, Geneva tr.). It seems plausible that the pamphlet came into being because of *The Fair Quarrel,* which demonstrated Middleton's concern over the question of dueling.

## CHAPTER 8

# *Tragedies*

DURING most of Middleton's career he did not write tragedies. He composed the lost *The Chester Tragedy* as early as October, 1602; and he alleged that in May, 1606, he delivered *The Viper and Her Brood* to Robert Keysar. *The Viper* (also lost) may have been a tragedy; some scholars believe it to be identical with *The Revenger's Tragedy* traditionally ascribed to Cyril Tourneur.[1] But for the next dozen years, so far as records tell, Middleton wrote no tragedies. Sometime between 1615 and 1620, perhaps about 1618, he either reshaped *Vortiger,* an old play, or found in Holinshed's *Chronicles* a story which he adapted as a tragedy, *The Mayor of Queenborough.* Probably his next tragedy was *Women Beware Women,* and finally he collaborated with William Rowley on *The Changeling* in early 1622. All three of his extant tragedies are dramas of lust and intrigue, and in all three the Jacobean interest in psychological analysis is vividly exhibited.

### I The Mayor of Queenborough

*The Mayor of Queenborough or Hengist, King of Kent* begins as a chronicle history, a type of drama no longer popular by 1618. Act I bears out the promise of the opening; in Act II, however, Middleton obscures the instructive purposes of the historical play by introducing material without political implications. This material, concerned with lust and amorous intrigues, dominates the rest of the play. Following the late Jacobean trend, *The Mayor of Queenborough* brings into the foreground episodes that are completely unhistorical and moves into the area of historical romance.[2]

Middleton used Holinshed's *Chronicles* as the main source for his play, which in broad outlines resembles *Macbeth* but which takes the reader back to post-Roman and pre-Saxon Britain. Ambitious Vortiger supplants Constantius, the rightful king, and, to maintain his power, Vortiger hires Saxons led by Hengist and Horsus. Overcome by lust, he then creates occasion to cast off his wife, Castiza (Holinshed said that he "forsooke his owne wife"), and marries Roxena, daughter of Hengist. She is already the mistress of Horsus, who continues to enjoy her favors while pretending to be the loyal friend and closest adviser of Vortiger. When the Britons rise against Vortiger for taking a pagan wife, they choose as king Vortiger's son Vortimer. After Vortimer is poisoned by Roxena, they accept Vortiger again as ruler; but they wish to expel the Saxons.

Driven by his ambition (ambition then meant inordinate desire to gain power, even by illegal means), Hengist the Saxon has his men treacherously attack the Britons at a parley; and he exacts Kent, Norfolk, and Suffolk as the price of Vortiger's liberty. After Hengist thus becomes king of Kent, the British besiege Vortiger and Roxena in a Welsh castle (Horsus is there, still cuckolding Vortiger). The play ends with the burning of the castle; the deaths of Vortiger, Roxena, and Horsus; and the capture by the British of Hengist. The play also includes a rather substantial subplot involving Simon the tanner, who becomes the mayor of Queenborough.

The historical material covers a period of years, much of which Middleton condenses by means of dumbshows and narrative choruses. The dramatist selects from his sources certain dramatic foci round which he organizes the play. He first stresses the contrast of Constantius and Vortiger; for, following a suggestion in Fabyan's chronicle, Middleton makes Constantius a deeply devout monk who most reluctantly leaves a monastery for a throne.[3] Vortiger, burning with ambition to rule, tortures Constantius with a series of necessary ordeals which the king hates but which Vortiger hopes will force him to abdicate. Vortiger even sends his own betrothed, Castiza, to try to tempt the king; and he finally hires murderers to kill Constantius. The king's brothers, Aurelius Ambrose, and Uther, like Duncan's sons in *Macbeth,* flee for safety. Then Vortiger forces Castiza to marry him. The people rise up, and he accepts Saxon aid to retain his throne.

Following Holinshed's statement that "the king was much giuen to sensuall lust," Middleton lets the theme of lust shape much of his play from Act II, Scene iii, on. He invents the affair between

Roxena and Horsus and uses it as the basis of a tense scene (II.iii). When Horsus swoons—overcome by the shock of hearing Vortiger create Hengist Duke of Kent in order to obtain Roxena for himself—Roxena says Horsus is troubled with epilepsy, which can be cured by "a virgins right hand stroakt vpon his heart" (1. 251). There is much suspense while she persuades Horsus not to reveal her shame as his mistress. When he rises, as if restored by her hand stroke, her credit is high with Vortiger. Using a plot suggested by Horsus, Vortiger rids himself of Castiza by making her think she has been abducted and raped when he has actually possessed her.[4] Then at a banquet he arranges to make her confess to her supposed dishonor, while Roxena, a pagan, boldly swears to her own purity. Thus Vortiger feels that he has given public satisfaction for rejecting Castiza and marrying Roxena.

Middleton draws on Holinshed for two other episodes of dramatic importance. First is the striking down of the Britons at the parley by the Saxons when they are told "Nemp your sexes!" (Draw your swords.) Consequently, Hengist is enabled to become King of Kent. Lastly comes the great spectacle of the burning of the stronghold of Vortiger. He attempts to deflect the British anger from himself to Horsus by informing the attackers that Horsus alone originated the intrigue against Queen Castiza and by offering them Horsus to appease them. He stabs Horsus; but Horsus retaliates with a wound to the soul by telling him the truth about false Roxena. Vortiger and Horsus kill each other while Roxena, pleading for succor, is burnt by the flames which appear to her in the form of poisoned Vortimer and which symbolize her raging lust. With the sentencing of the captive Hengist to death, *The Mayor of Queenborough* ends. Death is, therefore, the wages of sin—of lust and ambition. The play turns into melodrama, and there is scarcely another play of the period that has a more glaringly spectacular close.

In addition to sensationalism, the play has other shortcomings. It is not perfectly proportioned; the lust theme is so dilated that political and military matters must be represented in narrative or compressed with hasty action. A steady focus of interest on Vortiger as protagonist is lacking; rather, emphasis is parcelled out among Constantius, Hengist, and even Horsus. And part of the trouble is that the avengers have two usurpers to deal with, not one as in *Macbeth;* in the end, vengeance is taken by the British princes, whom one knows less than Malcolm in *Macbeth,* against Vortiger and then against Hengist.

Too much space is also devoted to the comic subplot. Probably the pride and petty tyranny exhibited by Simon the tanner after he becomes mayor were meant as a comic parallel to Vortiger's tyranny and hatred of the populace in the main action, and Simon's cheating by the actors, as a parallel to Vortiger's cheating by the Saxons. Excellent farce though the Simon matter is, the lengthy scene of the mayor's gulling (V.i) is a fatal interruption of the flow of the would-be tragic action. The play fails to attain a unity of purpose, action, and emotional quality.[5]

In spite of the lurid flame and gore of its sensational ending and in spite of the shift from political matters to the intrigues of the lust-driven triangle which dominate its second half, *The Mayor* has certain virtues recognized by recent critics:[6] the effectiveness of the characterizations, the power of the irony, and the excellence of the poetry. One of the reasons for Middleton's continued reputation is his psychological penetration of his characters. Taking the few clues the chroniclers provide for some characters and using only his own imagination for others, Middleton is able to create effective beings such as the pure Constantius and the ambitiously worldly and lustful Vortiger, Roxena, and Horsus.

Middleton generally finds human beings flawed by selfishness and hypocrisy. Constantius, however, is sincerely devout and unworldly. Even in a palace he remains a monk: he grieves that he wears fine clothes and that his attendants waste their time on him and do not think of their souls. Though there are touches of irony throughout the treatment of Constantius which create mildly grotesque humor, the characterization of the monk haled out of his cloister is, within its limits of scarcely 350 lines, very successfully imagined.

In one sense more conventional, since he is a Machiavellian villain (as is Hengist), Vortiger is a greater creation than Constantius; for he is more complex. A "Machiavel" lacks conscience and is often antireligious; filled with ambition for power, he ruthlessly destroys opponents by plots or by force. Vortiger, however, is not a typical Machiavel: he is too much influenced by sensuality, and he puts too easy trust in his Saxon allies. Professor Schoenbaum calls the characterization of Vortiger "a powerful study of a primitive and passionate man" (92). Middleton sees him as an unsophisticated person who, surprised by the variety and subtlety of a great new world, asks himself "How can such things be?" He muses, for example, as Constantius leaves the monastery:

> Can this greate motion of Ambition stand
> Like wheeles false wrought by an vnskilfull hand,
> Then time stand thou too, let no hopes ariue
> At their sweete wishfulness till mine sett forward,
> Wold I Could stay this existance; as I Can
> Thy glassy Counterfeit in hours of sand;
> Ide keepe the turnd downe till my wishes rose,
> Then weede both rise together;
> What seuerall inclinations are in nature:
> How much is he disquietted, and weares royaltie
> Disdainfullie vpon him like a Curse,
> Calls a faire Crowne the waight of his afflictions
> When heres a soule wold sing vnder that Burthen.
> (I.i.176–88)

Vortiger also seems surprised that, after attaining the kingship, he still retains the common pains and passions of the man he was: "haue I powre/Of life and death and Cannot Comand ease/In myne owne Blood: After I was a King/I thought I neuer shold haue felt paine more . . ." (III.i.96–99). And, though a usurper himself, he is shocked that ambitious Hengist has betrayed him (IV.iii.68–79).

Vortiger is conceived as a simple-minded fellow who selfishly drives ahead and who lacks the attributes of royalty; he is not capable of responsible kingship, to say nothing of his incapacity to rise to the role of a tragic hero. When Vortiger, looking down from his castle walls, begins to fear as he sees besiegers everywhere, he says, "Begirt all round." Horsus, who has more fortitude and a clearer vision, replies: "All all my Lord: tis folly to make doubt ont;/You question things that horror long agon/Resolud vs on" (V.ii.15–18). In contrast to Horsus' toughness is Vortiger's animal panic and his ignoble attempt to save his own skin by piling blame on Horsus and handing him over to the Britons.

As Barker and Schoenbaum have indicated, Horsus is a character more subtly drawn and intricate than Vortiger. As observer and actor—a sensualist capable of ironic detachment—he is a sort of bitter epicure at life's table. He too meditates on the life about him but with the cynical tone of experience, not with the primitive Vortiger's wonder; Vortiger is a countryman beside the knowing city sophisticate of Horsus. Horsus, who quickly constructs the scheme to destroy Castiza's reputation, carries it out skillfully; but he remains aloof enough to express pity for a woman so betrayed, and he has to contend with his own compassion when Castiza pleads for her honor (III.ii.98–106). Aware of the political consequences of Vortiger's choice of Roxena, Horsus appreciates the irony of her winning a contest for chastity. When Vortiger, like an old-time Senecan hero, indulges in self-pity (IV.iii.138–43), Horsus hypocritically vows friendship so he can be with Roxena. Middleton conceives for Horsus a strange infatuation with Roxena: he knows how lustful and deceitful she is, but he acquiesces in all she does so long as he can possess her. He represents a preliminary study for De Flores in *The Changeling*,[7] who is consumed with desire for Beatrice-Joanna; and who, having become one with her in lust and wickedness, dedicates himself to her. Horsus illustrates the Jacobean fascination with examining subtly varied types of depravity.

Roxena is another portrait in Middleton's gallery of beautiful, sensuous, and, above all, willful women. She resembles Francisca in *The Witch*, Eugenia in *The Old Law*, Aurelia in *More Dissemblers*, and Beatrice-Joanna in *The Changeling*. Middleton has, however, made her less blindly lustful and more perceptive than the others.

*The Mayor of Queenborough* is filled with examples of Middleton's irony: Hengist congratulates himself on Roxena's devotion, but her passion for Horsus has drawn her to Britain; Vortiger is surprised that kingship does not obliterate other passions, but he trusts Horsus as a friend and Roxena as a virgin. The deepest and bitterest irony pertains, however, to Castiza. She feels pleased that her marriage has been happier than she had hoped; she trusts in Vortiger's love—"It lasts and holds out long" (III.ii.20).[8] Immediately afterward Horsus with the king's approval seizes and blindfolds her. She invites him to take her life if he desires. The sharpest irony of the play is in his reply: " 'tis not life/That I thirst after, loyaltie forbid/I should comītt such Treason . . ." (III.ii.57–59).

Middleton's poetry in *The Mayor of Queenborough* is frequently of a high order. In addition to passages already quoted and the many distinguished single lines and brief passages, the eloquent words of Constantius commending chastity to Castiza deserve notice:

> Keep still that holy and im̄aculate fire
> You Chaste Lampe of eternitye, tis a treasure
> Too pretious for deaths moment to pertake,
> This twinckling of short life; Disdaine as much
> To lett mortality knowe you, as starrs
> To kiss y^e^ pauem^ts^, y'haue a substance
> As excellent as theirs, holding yo^r^ pureness;
> They looke vpon Coruption as you doe
> But are starrs still; be you a virgin too. (I.ii.179–87)

In quite a different key is the packed poetic power of Hengist's sententious urging that each Saxon bring a concealed dagger to the parley:

> Therefore be quick, dispatch, here every man
> Receive into thee service of his vengeance
> An instrument of steele, w^ch^ will vnseene,
> Lurke like y^e^ snake vnder y^e^ innocent shade
> Of a spread sommers leafe; and as greate substance
> Blocks itselfe vp into lesse roome in gold
> Then other mettles, and less Burthensome
> So in y^e^ other hand lyes all Confinde
> Full as much Death as ever changd mankind;
> Tis all y^e^ same time that a small watch showes
> As greate Church dialls & as true as those. (IV.iii.21–31)

The easy compacting and elaboration of imaged thought in the lines quoted show Middleton a great poet of the true Jacobean stamp; but it is easier to perceive the effect of his poetry than to analyze and explain it. Such a line as "Gallops downe hill as feareless as a drunkard" (II.iii.191) illustrates in brief the success attained in many more elaborated passages. Each passage cited has a mingling of simile and metaphor frequently providing a rich poetic texture, and the freshness and pungency of the images are reinforced by the connotations of supporting words.

Thus, in spite of its sensationalism and its structural deficiencies, *The Mayor of Queenborough* has elements of greatness that entitle it to be included, as Professor Schoenbaum says, "with the half dozen or so outstanding works" [9] of Middleton.

## II Women Beware Women

*Women Beware Women,* perhaps acted in 1621,[10] is a tragedy of Italianate intrigue. For his main plot Middleton used a version of the well-known story of Bianca Capello, probably that of Celio Malespini in his *Ducento Novelli* (Venice, 1609). Bianca, beautiful daughter of a great family of Venice, became infatuated with a young Florentine, Pietro Buonaventuri, who worked in a Venetian bank. Faced with discovery of their secret affair, they fled to Florence and poverty; for Pietro was of humble birth. Bianca, however, endured her lot patiently because of her love. When the Grand Duke Francesco de' Medici happened to see her at her window, he was attracted by her beauty; and, when he had found out about her misfortunes, he persuaded her to come to his palace with the help of a Spaniard and his wife, Mandragona. The wife gave Bianca a tour of the palace and brought her to the waiting Francesco. Bianca begged for pity and the Duke assured her of his aid. Soon, however, she became his mistress. Pietro, the acquiescent husband, was taken care of with wealth and advancement at court.

After a time Pietro became wild and arrogant; he boasted of his affair with the widow Cassandra and finally made himself so obnoxious that the Duke left him to the vengeance of Cassandra's nephew Roberto. After Pietro's death, the Duke married Bianca, his first wife being dead. From some other source, Middleton utilized material about the deaths of Bianca and the Duke. Her attempt to have her child by Francesco legitimized was opposed by Cardinal Ferdinand, the Duke's brother. When she attempted to poison the cardinal, the Duke by mistake ate of the poisoned food; and she deliberately ate it also, joining her husband in death.

Middleton's subplot is based on a French tale, *Des amours tragiques, et estranges adventures d'Hypolite & Isabelle Neapolitains* by one Sieur Meslier (Paris, 1610). In this story of enforced marriage, Isabella's father, Fabritio, wished to marry his beautiful daughter to a foolish son of the girl's stepmother, Livia, on account of the young man's wealth. Isabella hated the foolish, repulsive Pompeio; but she fell in love with her uncle Hippolito, a handsome young man equally attracted to her. They could not free themselves of this guilty love; and, when Hippolito explained his situation to his sister, a nun, she, out of pity for him, informed Isabella that not Fabritio but the Marquess of Coria was her father. Isabella and Hippolito then became lovers, and she married Pompeio. The affair of the guilty couple was made known to Pompeio's guardian, who persecuted them and brought about the death of Isabella. Hippolito's vengeance was thwarted by the guardian's death, but Hippolito killed Pompeio. Later he too met an unhappy death.[11]

Probably Middleton chose to combine these two stories of thrilling sexual passion because they exhibit such pronounced contrasts on the theme of marriage. Bianca's story represents an extreme of romantic, unenforced marriage; Isabella's, the bitterest extreme of mercenary, enforced marriage. Lust—reinforced by greed, vanity, and willfulness—brings about the downfall of all the characters.

To dramatize the stories in a unified plot, Middleton confronted formidable problems of plotting. His finest stroke in solving these problems was to combine into a single character the functions of the Spaniard's wife, Mandragona; Isabella's stepmother, Livia; Hippolito's sister, the nun; and the widow Cassandra. This character is Fabricio's sister Livia, a wealthy widow at ease in court circles, who is also Isabella's aunt, Hippolito's sister, and the landlady of the foolish ward and his guardian (Guardiano). Guardiano replaces the Spaniard as the Duke's friend and agent in seduction, and Hippolito has the avenging function of Cassandra's nephew. Thus Middleton efficiently reduced the number of characters in his sources from seventeen to eleven for his play.

In the play, Bianca's husband is called Leantio and is given a business as a "factor" or Renaissance traveling salesman. The young couple live with his poor old mother, whose house is close to Livia's; and, as in the city comedies, the action is a neighborhood affair. Livia invites the mother in for "Thursday supper" and "Sunday dinner" and plays chess with her from time to time.

Middleton opens his drama *in medias res* with the arrival of the eloping couple at Leantio's mother's house. Leantio overflows with pride in his wife's beauty, the "treasure" that he has stolen and that will keep him from lustful indulgence, and he glories in his theft. His mother stresses prudential considerations; she chides

Leantio for recklessly separating the girl from normal expectations of fortune and reminds him that he has scarcely been able to support himself:

> What ableness have you to do her right then
> In maintenance fitting her birth and virtues?
> Which every woman of necessity looks for,
> And most to go above it, not confin'd
> By their conditions, virtues, bloods, or births,
> But flowing to affections, wills, and humours.
> (I.i.65–70)

Leantio, who brushes aside her premonitory analysis, relies on Bianca's honeymoon love and obedience to make her content with his low fortunes and not to follow "the licentious swing of her own will" (I.i.52). Meanwhile, he hopes to prosper by hard work. Only by the utmost effort of will, however, can he tear himself from her to go on a five-day business trip. Bianca does not encourage him to leave, as a thrifty wife might; she begs him to remain another night. Leantio knows what a relaxing of will power his giving in would lead to. For all of his selfishness and sensuality, he is superior to Bianca in holding certain principles on discipline in love and marriage:

> . . . love that's wanton must be rul'd awhile
> By that that's careful, or all goes to ruin:
> As fitting is a government in love
> As in a kingdom; where 'tis all mere lust,
> 'Tis like an insurrection in the people. . . . (I.iii.41–45)

Leantio leaves reluctantly, insisting that Bianca must be kept unseen in the house lest Florentine gallants try to seduce her.

Immediately chance gives their marriage a stiff blow. The mother chides Bianca a bit for enticing Leantio to remain home; and the girl, alone for the first time among strangers in an old mean house and thwarted of her will, breaks into weeping. Since the old woman has not meant to hurt her, she is the more willing to make her daughter-in-law happy by showing her the procession just about to pass the house, the "yearly custom and solemnity" in which she can see the Duke, "a goodly gentleman of his years" (I.iii.93). As the Duke passes, Bianca thinks he has looked at them. The mother doubts it; everyone supposes a Duke looks at him, whereas the Duke is probably thinking of "his own intentions, and his object/Only the public good" (I.iii.113–14). This speech is dramatic irony; for though the Duke, having glimpsed Bianca, does have his own intentions, his object is emphatically not public good. Thus, by the end of Act I, Middleton has set forth the opening situation of the main action and the initial incident leading to complications.

In Act I, Scene ii, Middleton introduces the subplot, first emphasizing Isabella's bitter objection to marrying the foolish Ward of Fabricio and her dilemma, caught between loathing for the Ward and her duty to obey her mercenary father. Then tormented Hippolito reveals to Isabella his incestuous feelings. He acknowledges the iniquity of incest: ". . . heaven has forbid it;/And 'tis most meet that I should rather perish/Than the decree divine receive least blemish" (I.ii.156–58). Isabella is shocked, and she sends him away, grieved because "blood, that should be love, is mix'd with lust" (I.ii.231).

In the first scene of Act II good-natured, amoral Livia assures Hippolito that she can arrange to satisfy his sensuality. He is dubious; she, feeling pride in her capacities of scheming and manipulation, is the more eager to show what she can do. She then relates to Isabella the false tale of her illegitimate birth, with many cautions to observe secrecy. The cleverest touch is the way in which she tells Isabella not to inform Hippolito of this story: "And though you love him dearly, as I know/His deserts claim as much even from a stranger/ [that is, *you are not of his blood*] Yet let him not know this . . ." (II.i.172–74).

Livia has informed Isabella: "I told you I should start your blood" (II.i.134). This statement has a double meaning: (1) give a tremendous surprise; (2) rouse the passions. Once the dread of incest is removed, the girl's passion for Hippolito springs forth; and she sees the marriage as a convenient concealment for an affair. She regrets only that she did not know the "truth" a day earlier so that she might not have given Hippolito pain.[12] She begs his forgiveness for rejecting him and reveals her change of heart with one of Middleton's richest, most vivid metaphors. The play is filled with figures of food and eating, but none is more notable than this one:

When we invite our best friends to a feast,
'Tis not all sweetmeats that we set before them;
There's somewhat sharp and salt, both to whet appetite
And make 'em taste their wine well; so, methinks,
After a friendly, sharp and savoury chiding,
A kiss tastes wondrous well, and full o' the grape. . . .
(II.i.198–203)

The next scene of the main plot, the long Act II, Scene ii, is the famous seduction scene. Guardiano enlists Livia's cleverness, with the enticement of "wealth and favour" from the Duke; but she is put on her mettle by the need for cunning manipulation in which she takes such pride. So she sends for Leantio's mother as a neighbor and hears the news that she has a young gentlewoman at home—whom she immediately invites also, and Bianca is sent for. The mother's scruples are overborne by the initiative of Livia, who is of higher station; the mother does not wish to displease her affable friend. The mother has no inkling of doing ill, though she is aware that Leantio will be angry if he finds out that she has let Bianca leave home.

When Bianca arrives, she is welcomed most warmly. All through this part of the scene there is an overdone, or overacted, gentility in the speeches of Livia and Guardiano; the affability is so great that the visitors feel they must rise to the occasion. While Livia and the mother play chess, Guardiano shows Bianca about the house to see the "rooms and pictures." The tour is represented as a genteel attempt to entertain a young person who probably lacks "patience/To look upon two weak and tedious gamesters" (II.ii.273–74). This scene is one of Middleton's greatest ironic successes. Bianca is sent to see the sights, "the monument too, and that's a thing/Every one sees not" (II.ii.282–83). Her later comments about the tour and the conversation of the chess players while it takes place constitute brilliant irony.

When she is left with the Duke, he uses against her his greatness, hints of force and power held in abeyance, his admiration of her beauty, and finally the temptation of wealth and high place with lifelong security which contrasts, of course, to her present poverty and insecurity:

And can you be so much your beauty's enemy,
To kiss away a month or two in wedlock,

> And weep whole years in wants for ever after?
> Come, play the wise wench, and provide for ever. . . .
> (II.ii.384–87)

Bianca is seduced mainly, it seems, by the vision of wealth.[13]

Her temptation takes place *above*—that is, on an "upper stage" —and from time to time Livia (and the mother in her ignorance) make comments about the chess game which have an ironic meaning in relation to the Duke's game taking place upstairs. After Bianca has retired with her new protector, Livia says, "I've given thee blind mate twice," and a bit later, "The game's even at the best now. . . . Has not my duke bestirr'd himself?" (II.ii.397, 414, 419).

The initiation into sin causes a transformation of Bianca; as she says, she is emboldened—to curse Guardiano and to call Livia, in an aside, a "damn'd bawd." With bitter sarcasm, she explains to the blindly complacent mother what she has seen:

> The monument and all: I'm so beholding
> To this kind, honest, courteous gentleman,
> You'd little think it, mother; show'd me all,
> Had me from place to place so fashionably;
> The kindness of some people, how't exceeds!
> Faith, I've seen that I little thought to see
> I' the morning when I rose. (II.ii.456–62)

The juxtaposition here of guilty knowledge, secret and betrayed, with ignorant bland complacency produces irony of extraordinary wryness. Though Livia is momentarily pricked by Bianca's charge, she lays it to her greenness—"Being not accustom'd to the breaking billow/Of woman's wavering faith blown with temptations: . . . /Sin tastes at the first draught like wormwood-water,/ But drunk again, 'tis nectar ever after" (II.ii.478–82). Livia well knows what changes sophistication and experience bring about.

Five days later the mother is wearied beyond patience at the "most sudden'st, strangest alteration" (III.i.63) in Bianca. All her prognostications of a rich girl's dissatisfaction have come true; Bianca is querulous, petulant, and spiteful; and this is the day of Leantio's return. Since "Honest wedlock/Is like a banqueting-house built in a garden," (III.i.89–90), he is anticipating greedy love from his wife. Her change astounds him; she treats him like a cold woman of fashion: "Think of the world, how we shall live; grow serious;/We have been married a whole fortnight now" (III.i.166–67). He makes her retire while he talks to a messenger from the Duke who is inviting her to a banquet at Livia's. Leantio stalls the messenger, and then addresses his wife. Though he does not know it, his words have a double meaning that frightens Bianca: "Thou art betray'd, I fear me. . . ./The Duke knows thee" (III.i.206–7). She and the mother conceal their visit to Livia's, but the mother tells her son that the Duke probably saw Bianca at the window while the procession was passing. When Leantio declares that he will lock Bianca in a special hiding place "at the end of the dark parlour," Bianca declares that he must be out of his mind: "What's the matter?" He cries, "Why, are you so insensible of your danger/To ask that now? the Duke himself has sent for you/To Lady Livia's to a banquet, forsooth" (III.i.252–54).

With these words, Leantio has toppled his world about his head; for, infuriated at him, Bianca rushes to the banquet; and his mother is of Bianca's mind: "I'll first obey the Duke,/And taste of a good banquet" (III.i.275–76). The mother's mind is on literal sweetmeats; Bianca's, on the sweets of illicit love and grandeur. Leantio is left to reverse his sentiments about marriage: "O thou, the ripe time of man's misery, wedlock/. . . . What a peace/Has he that never marries!" In his earlier speech, he had praised "honest wedlock" and deprecated the "glorious dangerous strumpet"; now he envies the man "That wears his youth out in a strumpet's arms . . ." (III.i.271, 280–81, 287). Then he too is invited to the banquet, and his disillusionment is completed in the next scene.

Act III, Scene ii, though less brilliant in irony than the seduction scene, is a fine achievement. Middleton here brings his two plots together, for the Ward and his man Sordido are at the banquet to consider whether Isabella will make the Ward a suitable wife. The scene is focused mainly, however, on the sufferings of Leantio. The Duke has openly taken Bianca as his favorite; and, to prevent trouble with Leantio, he tosses him a post as captain of a fort. Hurt, outraged, and yet, in spite of himself, gratified, Leantio feels that he is suffering retribution for his theft of Bianca (III.ii.94–95). Middleton clearly understands the reactions of this victimized member of the lower bourgeoisie among aristocrats and gentry. They are all gay, having sport with the Ward, while miserable Leantio looks on. Much of the scene is ironic comedy.

During the banquet, Livia suddenly falls in love with Leantio. For the sake of the plot to come, they have to be brought together. When the Duke takes Bianca away, Leantio is desperately near a breakdown; while he looked on her, he "half enjoy'd" her, and he can scarcely give up all hope of her.

> O hast thou left me then, Bianca, utterly?. . . .
> . . . 'tis an affliction
> Of greater weight than youth was made to bear;
> As if a punishment of after-life
> Were faln upon man here, so new it is
> To flesh and blood, so strange, so insupportable. . . .
> (II.ii.241–48)

There is great dramatic irony in his speech as Livia approaches him: "This cannot be but of some close bawd's working" (III.ii.267). He refuses to admit, when Livia tells him, that Bianca is a strumpet; and he has to use all his power to force himself to hate her in order to retain his sanity. Finally, Livia returns and offers him wealth, fine clothes, pleasures, and her love. The temptation of wealth and grandeur seduced Bianca; the parallel one from Livia seduces Leantio.

Middleton understands how physical attraction can so possess a person that he cannot keep away from the loved one. Livia, when she begins to love Leantio, has "not power/To keep from sight of him" (III.i.349–50); and Leantio still feels a compulsion to see Bianca[14] although it is compounded with curiosity, envy, and spite. In this fashion Middleton adapts the troublemaking of Pietro in his source to perform a crucially important function in his plot.

The events in Act IV, Scene i, in which Leantio visits Bianca at court, are founded in his character: the injured, discarded husband now makes a fine appearance; cannot resist flaunting his finery before the splendid strumpet that Bianca has become; spitefully taunts her; and, out of hurt pride, advertises his own love success. She has the better of the set-to; and he becomes infuriated with her, calling her names and handing her a letter to read—"thou shalt find there I'm not love-starv'd" (IV.i.67)—which informs her that he has a liaison with Livia. In terms of the action, the whole point of their quarrel is to provide her with this information.

Leantio's injury and outrage are so great that he preaches and threatens. The last speech he tumbles out before he leaves contains some of Middleton's most condensed poetry:

> Why do I talk to thee of sense or virtue,
> That art as dark as death? and as much madness
> To set the light before thee, as to lead blind folks
> To see the monuments, which they may smell as soon
> As they behold. . . .
> So to an ignorance darker than thy womb
> I leave thy perjur'd soul; a plague will come!
> (IV.i.95–99, 105–5)

Leantio, the wronged husband, is thus self-righteous; but Bianca, refusing to acknowledge any justification for his grief and anger, takes refuge in sneering at this "poor, base start-up" with his vulgar display and his vulgar scolding. She even calls him "the former thing" (IV.i.114).

Stung to outrage, Bianca tells the Duke that Livia is now the mistress of her husband. She tells him, too, of Leantio's threats. The Duke assures her that all shall be well. How far ahead the Duke is planning at this point one cannot be sure; immediately, however, to give peace to Bianca, he tells Hippolito of Livia's defection, knowing that Hippolito has a keen sense of family honor; and, to impel him the more, he also tells Hippolito that he has a great match in mind for his sister. Shocked, the zealous Hippolito cries: "O thou destruction of all happy fortunes,/Unsated blood!" (IV.i.161–62). In his ignorance, he cannot feel the dramatic irony of his sententious speech. He determines, out of love for Livia, to use the knife, like a surgeon, and cure her honor.[15]

The Duke is now assailed by his brother the Cardinal, who tries to bring him to a sense of shame, duty, and religion. The Duke asserts his repentance and vows that he will not "keep woman more, unlawfully" (IV.i.256); but he equivocates, for he knows that Leantio will soon be dead and that he can marry Bianca. A chain of events is, therefore, inexorably linked: Bianca betrays Leantio, Leantio consoles himself with Livia and, out of spite, boasts to Bianca that Livia is his "beauteous benefactor," Bianca tells the Duke, the Duke tells Hippolito, and Hippolito kills Leantio because he loves his sister's "good so dearly, that no brother/Shall venture farther for a sister's glory/Than I for her preferment" (IV.ii.18–20).

The killing of Leantio draws a crowd: the Ward and Sordido, Guardiano, Isabella, and Livia. When she sees her beloved Leantio dead, Livia, filled with bitterness and rage, flings in her brother's face that dreadful secret of "the black lust 'twixt thy niece and thee . . ." (IV.ii.67). The others hear her too. Isabella cannot endure the guilt of incest; and she turns from her lover. Since Livia feels that she is receiving retribution for her sin, her feelings parallel those of Leantio earlier. But she hates her brother now as the murderer of her "love's joy," and Guardiano and the Ward desire revenge upon him for his abuse of Isabella. Hippolito ruefully realizes that he has destroyed his own happiness with his niece. The irony that a man living in incest acts to save family honor is doubled by the irony that his well-intended action recoils upon himself. Though Isabella, Guardiano, and Livia dissemble their hatreds, they plan vengeance under cover of a wedding masque for the Duke.

Since Middleton has eliminated Bianca's child (in fact, he has telescoped some twenty-five years of history into a few months at most[16] of dramatic time), he has to invent a reason for Bianca's hatred of the Cardinal; and he does so by having the Cardinal confront the Duke and Bianca on their way to the altar and accuse his brother of hypocrisy and deliberate sin in marrying the strumpet he had seemingly renounced. The Duke sticks by the letter of his promise, and Bianca accuses the Cardinal of judging uncharitably instead of delighting in her becoming a lawful wife and thus, as she implies, "a converted sinner" (IV.iii.56). The Cardinal's words which end Act IV are ominous in their coupling of lust and vengeance: "Lust is bold,/And will have vengeance ere't be controll'd" (IV.iii.71–72). The Cardinal's opposition to the marriage and his alleged envy, since he is heir to the dukedom, provide motives for Bianca's hatred and her decision to murder him.

During the masque Isabella, Livia, Guardiano, and Hippolito are destroyed. Meanwhile, Bianca has poisoned wine for the Cardinal, but it is mistakenly drunk by the Duke, and, upon realizing the situation, she drinks the remainder to join him in death. Hippolito is given some insight and a dying-moment opportunity to explain the machinations: "Lust and forgetfulness has been amongst us,/And we are brought to nothing . . ." (V.i.187–88). Bianca voices the ostensible theme of the play: "O, the deadly snares/That women set for women. . . ./Like our own sex we have no enemy" (V.i.253–57).

In terms of its title and of its source, one expects Bianca to be the central character of the drama; but, if tragedy is "the artistic presentation of human suffering," [17] Leantio is the character who suffers most and with whom the reader is likely to feel a modicum of sympathy. As it is, interest is dispersed among too many characters.[18] If this impressive play had been entitled *All's Lost by Lust,* many readers would probably feel better satisfied.

For the first four acts of *Women Beware Women,* Middleton organized his material in a tightly knit plot. His one remaining problem was to contrive punishment for the sinning characters, who, except for Duke, mother, and Cardinal, are seething with hatred. The "history" that Middleton followed dictated the means of death for the Duke and Bianca; but, according to Jacobean convention as well as Middleton's own moral convictions, the other erring characters also had to die. Since he had chosen the marriage as the reason for the Cardinal's intervention and as the final episode in Bianca's fortunes, the other deaths in the last act had to be related to the marriage.

Therefore, in all likelihood, he resolved to use the revenge-masque as the easiest way out of his difficulty, even though the device would seem old-fashioned since it had been used as far back as 1587 in Thomas Kyd's *The Spanish Tragedy.* Middleton has received some harsh criticisms for his last act, but it is difficult to see how a practical playwright could have better solved the problem. Those who disapprove of the device itself must realize that changing the last act would entail other changes also because both acts IV and V are built upon the marriage. Without the masque, *Women Beware Women* would have to be a far different play. It is hard to see what other device short of sinking a ship or burning a house could cause so many deaths in little more than two hundred lines.

Even so, one may of course take exception to the author's handling of Act V, and it is true that the style, somewhat changed, becomes more formal and less charged with irony and tension; too, it lacks the brilliant "naturalism," as it is usually called, of the earlier acts. As soon as Middleton decided to use a play-within-the-play, he could no longer write in a naturalistic mode. Barker and Ribner are right in seeing ritualism and symbolism in the stylized handling of Act V.[19] And, though, in general, the emotional drive of the play has slackened here and though the writing has less distinction, one should note a few flashes of extremely effective poetry (V.i.187–97; 242–50).

Although the abstract plot scheme of the play is well designed since the two wife-husband-lover triangles are united by Livia as a seducer, *Women Beware Women* does have some weaknesses of dramaturgy. First, the two plots are poorly balanced; the main plot requires so much space that the story of Isabella and Hippolito, after first being set up, receives only sketchy portrayal. Second, Middleton falls into the same fault he had committed in *The Mayor of Queenborough*—he gives too much attention to comedy: to the secondary figures of the subplot, to the smutty silliness of the Ward and Sordido. Third, the Cardinal, the only exponent of virtue in the play, appears very late in it. Although his speech of reproof in Act IV, Scene i, is thrillingly fine, he is no more than the agent of the author's thesis.

Not only is the last act moralistic but Middleton takes pains throughout the play to keep before the reader the moral consequences of the deeds portrayed. The key words of the drama are *lust, ruin,* and *destruction.* Mention of lust is pervasive, from Leantio's second speech—"as if lust went to market still on Sundays" (I.i.34)—to the last line of the play. *Ruin* and *destruction* stand both for moral downfall and for death, or even for death and damnation.[20] Middleton stresses the moral risks that his characters run. Thus, because "its themes are nearer to a thesis," *Women Beware Women* is less great than *The Changeling.*[21]

Nevertheless, *Women Beware Women* is for several reasons one of Middleton's finest achievements and a drama of great distinction. Foremost is the psychological penetration with which the characters are created and made to act. Leantio is perhaps the best understood; with his pride in his beauteous conquest, he is so engulfed with the pleasure he takes in Bianca that he is tempted to abandon his work: "Why should I toil my youth out?" (I.iii.18). He feels, however, the tug between pleasure and business; and, as a proper bourgeois, he blames himself for being tempted by irresponsibility. He is imprudent, uxorious, and rather shallow; but he acts after the nature of many untried young men. And he is no stoic, for Livia, the lady from the world of the court, overbears him in his lonely moment with enticement of love and security. Thoroughly plausible, too, is the conversion of Leantio's infatuation into the pride and angry spite that lead to his undoing.

Middleton's knowledge of feminine psychology for which he has become famous enables him to create the three women who very nearly equal the characterization of Leantio: the mother, Bianca, and Livia. The mother has picked up a kind of aphoristic fund of knowledge about human nature, and it appears rather like prudence; but, because of her lowly position, she is stupidly impressed by the pretensions of her superiors. She finds Bianca's complaining about the lack of elegance and luxury in her house incomprehensible. This complaining is one of the best strokes in the portrait of Bianca; for the rich girl, now awakened once more to "the ambitions to which she was entitled, emerges from the negative." [22] Her seduction by the world and the flesh hardens and energizes her until she flies on sinful, willful wings far above the dull chrysalis of poverty in which she had ignorantly immured herself. With all her shortcomings and her shallowness, Bianca is as real a character as Flaubert's Emma Bovary or as Tolstoy's Anna Karenina.

Livia contrasts to these characters who can be called ignorant, stupid, or blind. A clever woman, she takes pride in her cunning. Although she seems to have some regard for the right, it is not strong enough to restrain her from self-indulgence and machination. Middleton gives her a warm persuasive power that goes with her great vitality and free-and-easy nature; she acts the role of hearty, abundant friendship—but it comes from her heart, without malice. Although the social distance is great, she can bear comparison, for vitality, with La Celestina, the unforgettable bawd of the Spanish *Calisto and Meliboea.*

Like other Middleton characters, but more realistically portrayed, these willful people are driven by impulses, desires, and lusts. They have no concept of moderation or of stoical endurance. They must act. More than Middleton's other plays, *Women Beware Women* reveals how ready human beings are to accept any accommodation, any slippery adaptation of the moral code, in order to obtain with the least pain and trouble that which their temperaments drive them to seek.

The second distinction of the play is the sureness with which Middleton represents class structure and social conventions. The ruler of this society is the Duke, who employs his great power for self-indulgence and self-protection. He knows well what levers of greed, ambition, and "honor" to pull in order to operate the social machine. The people of the court have no moral sensitivity; theirs is a sensuous world of wealth and display based upon mercenary considerations. Fabricio and Guardiano are the most openly mercenary (Isabella is treated by both as an article of merchandise), but Livia is tempted into the seduction of Bianca partly by the hope of "wealth and favour," and even Leantio cannot help being flattered by his appointment as captain of a fort. In this indulgent, decadent world, anything can be arranged if one keeps quiet about it (IV.ii.8–9). The splendid appearance this world presents cloaks moral corruption (Middleton's "destruction") within. Leantio's world of the lesser bourgeoisie is sophisticated by the world above. Humility and deference are converted into snobbish hopes and fears that are quickly corrupted by the aristocrats.

The third special excellence of the play is the rendering of Middleton's main tragic theme: the effect of sin upon a person who has not encountered it before and who has not taken sufficient stock of himself to realize what his own nature is. Bianca begs the Duke: "Make me not bold with death and deeds of ruin"; but, after she has agreed to "take hold of glory," she returns changed: "sin and I'm acquainted,/No couple greater" (II.ii.356, 379, 444–45). Like Macbeth, Middleton's protagonists feel the progressively hardening effect of sin; but Bianca particularly exemplifies (like Beatrice in *Changeling*) "that degeneracy in character from acquiescence in sin to active wickedness that leads to violent death." [23] In a less spectacular way, Leantio also is worsened by his contact with the court.

Fourth and lastly, *Women Beware Women* is notable for its poetry. The fine, flexible verse of *A Chaste Maid* is perfected until it is capable in this play of unobtrusively achieving all purposes (except the most lyrical) of dramatic dialogue.[24] In the seduction scene the Duke's lines (for example, II.ii.332–38) have a rapid movement and a colloquial, quasi-bantering tone thoroughly appropriate to his world of fashion and sophistication. The result of the episode is neatly conveyed in the double meaning of the images of struggling for freedom.[25] The lines in which the Cardinal chides his brother (for example, IV.i.229–50), parrying the Duke's defense in his own worldly terms, have an effect of logic, coming from arrangement and enforced by contrasts; then the appeal becomes more serious, with a hortatory tone, stronger pauses, and heavier stresses. In this play, Middleton achieves a poetry without intense color that is, however, for dramatic purposes compact, powerful, and extremely suitable, much like Shakespeare's poetry in *Coriolanus*.

## III The Changeling

The greatest dramatic achievement of Middleton and Rowley, *The Changeling*, a tragedy licensed for acting on May 7, 1622, has its sources in new works that the authors had read not long before composing their play. The most important source is *The Triumphs of Gods Revenge against the Crying and Execrable Sinne of Willful and Premeditated Murther* by John Reynolds, a collection of exceedingly moralistic stories published after June 7, 1621. Reynolds tells his stories clumsily, for he is intent only on communicating the moral that murder cannot be hidden but that it will always be revealed and God's justice eventually accomplished. The authors recognized possibilities for a tragedy in History IV of Reynolds's Book I, a heavy-handed account of love, murder, and adultery in Spain which provides the framework for the main plot. To this story was welded material from Leonard Digges's *Gerardo the Unfortunate Spaniard*, a translation of a Spanish romance licensed for printing March 11, 1622.[26] *The Changeling* also has a subplot, for which no exact source has been identified although a part resembles the pursuit of Rebecca Purge by two gallants in Middleton's early *The Family of Love*.[27]

One imagines that Middleton and Rowley planned carefully in the spring of 1622 how to put dramatic life into their tragedy and that they then composed it in a fever of inspiration that finally resulted in this brilliant climax of their collaboration. The play was first acted by the Lady Elizabeth's Men at the *Phoenix;* and it received the honor on January 4, 1624, of a court performance. It was popular until the closing of the theaters in 1642, and it was revived after the Restoration. Audiences especially enjoyed the comic figure of the Changeling (Antonio) in the subplot.[28]

*The Changeling* is a product of close collaboration; whichever author was holding the pen, the effects in all parts were carefully devised. Nevertheless, the study of the internal evidence in the text reveals a clear division of the shares of the two authors. Rowley wrote acts I; III.iii; IV.iii; and V.iii. Middleton wrote acts II; III.i,ii,iv; IV.i,ii; and V.i,ii. Middleton handled most of the main plot; Rowley, practically all of the subplot. But Rowley opened the play with the main plot and brought both plots to a close in the last scene. This division of the writing is evidenced by differences of verbal habits, of versification, and of characterization. Middleton's fancy for the interjection "Push," for certain abstract terms, and for potent irony; his interest in such character types as the heroine and villain of the main plot; and his flexible blank verse with many feminine endings—all stand in contrast to Rowley's liking for puns, his use of a latinized vocabulary, his clumsy blank verse, and his interest in creating humorous clown characters such as Lollio and Antonio of the subplot.[29]

As the play opens, Alsemero, a young Valencian, delays his departure from Alicant for Malta because he has fallen in love for the first time in his life. He is infatuated with a beautiful girl he has seen in the church—a meeting place he regards as a good omen. She is Beatrice-Joanna, daughter of Vermandero, commander of the castle. After a kiss or two, a little gallantry, and some love talk, she regrets that Alsemero has appeared too late—only five days after her father has contracted her to Alonzo de Piracquo. Alsemero is invited to visit Vermandero's castle. Brushing aside his daughter's demurrer over marrying within a week, her father relishes the thought of having Piracquo for son-in-law: "I'll want/My will else." Her aside reveals her willful nature: "I shall want mine if you do it" (I.i.222–23).

In addition to the sudden, blazing love which has caused Beatrice to change her mind, the first scene reveals that she loathes "as a deadly poison" (I.i.114) an ugly gentleman who serves her father, De Flores. De Flores, who cannot keep away from Beatrice, is possessed by the thought of possessing her. When she drops a glove, she throws the other one down rather than take the first from De Flores. The authors stress greatly her antipathy to De Flores, who in the source is simply a young gallant. With the gloves in his hand—a lady's favor given with bitter disdain—De Flores muses:

Here's a favour come with a mischief now! I know
She had rather wear my pelt tann'd in a pair
Of dancing pumps, than I should thrust my fingers
Into her sockets here: I know she hates me,
Yet cannot choose but love her: no matter:
If but to vex her, I will haunt her still;
Though I get nothing else, I'll have my will. (I.i.235–40)

So Vermandero's will is for Beatrice to marry Piracquo, whereas her will is set on having Alsemero, and De Flores wills to have her himself. Also during the scene (in preparation for later plot needs) Alsemero's traveling companion Jasperino courts Beatrice's woman Diaphanta.

Alonzo de Piracquo willfully ignores the warning of his brother Tomazo that Beatrice appears not to love him. Ironically, under the circumstances, Alonzo feels a complacent "security": he cannot think that Beatrice even knows the meaning of inconstancy, "much less the use and practice" (II.i.148). He would like to marry her at once, but he agrees to a three-day postponement of the wedding.

Middleton retains from the source Beatrice's secret meeting with Alsemero and the kissing and embracing of the lovers. According to Reynolds, Beatrice tells Alsemero that "before *Piracquo* be in another world, there is no hope for *Alsemero* to injoy her for his wife in this" one. "Passion and affection blinding his judgment, and beautie triumphing and giving a law to his Conscience," Alsemero says that "hee will shortly send him a Challenge, and fight with him. . . ." [30] But the girl does not want Alsemero to hazard his life. The situation is the same in the play: Beatrice fears to lose Alsemero by the sword or by the law; but "Blood-guiltiness becomes a fouler visage . . ." (II.ii.40).

At this point in the play (the incident is not in the source), she thinks of the sinister ugliness of De Flores. De Flores himself has said that she treats him "as if danger or ill luck hung in my looks" (II.i.36). She feels harm and danger coming toward her every time she sees him. His presence exasperates her, infuriates her—until she suddenly changes her manner, having decided to buy at "so good a market" (II.ii.42). This change is the more ironic because, not long before, she had abused him and thought of wheedling her father into dismissing him.

Middleton greatly speeds up Reynolds' leisurely narrative, for

De Flores appears immediately after Alsemero's departure. He has spied on their meeting, hoping that, if Beatrice should prove false with Alsemero, her defection with himself will be more likely. (He has much the spirit of Horsus in *The Mayor of Queenborough.*) When Beatrice, making a show of interest in him, promises to treat his loathsome pimples and even touches his face with her own hand, he is enraptured. He soon learns that she needs the service of a resolute man to kill Alonzo. All the while he is thinking of her body: Middleton has him parody her words with coarse innuendos on "creation," "makes me man," "service," "mounts," and "act" (II.ii.92–133).[31] When De Flores understands that she desires Alonzo's death, he knows at once that he will gain his reward, his desire: "it will be precious; the thought ravishes!" (II.ii.133)

Middleton's irony is pervasive. Beatrice, willing to pay well and assuming that De Flores will leave the country, blinds herself to realities; her complacency produces strong dramatic irony as she congratulates herself that she will be rid "Of two inveterate loathings at one time . . ." (II.ii.147). Middleton condenses the action by having Alonzo request De Flores to show him the fortifications of the castle. As they traverse the passages and vaults, they talk of the wonders of the fort; and De Flores' speeches drip of irony: "All this is nothing; you shall see anon/A place you little dream on" (III.ii.1–2). Then De Flores treacherously kills him and cuts off a finger to get a diamond ring that will prove he has done the job.

Beatrice, meanwhile, commends herself for judgment and wisdom: "I've got him [Alsemero] now the liberty of the house;/So wisdom, by degrees, works out her freedom . . ." (III.iv.12–13). Dramatic irony soon reveals how fatuous the girl is; she is not working out her freedom but her bondage; and her "wisdom" is truly folly. She perceives her true situation during her conversation with De Flores, who immediately enters to report. Their interview is one of the greatest scenes in all drama.

Tears of joy spring to her eyes when she hears the favorable news, but she recoils when she sees Alonzo's finger: "Bless me, what hast thou *done?*" (III.iv.29). In one respect, Beatrice resembles Lady Macbeth: she has not visualized the act of murder. Murder was a way out of trouble that a clever person could arrange; she did not *see* it with eyes of realization. To De Flores her qualm seems absurd—to shudder at a finger when she has effected a murder. Scoffingly, he places the two acts in a more reasonable perspective: "I cut his heart-strings:/A greedy hand thrust in a dish at court,/In a mistake hath had as much as *this*" (III.iv.31–33 [italics added in this paragraph]).

The callousness of De Flores gives her the first hint that she is in a dirty business. The diamond on Alonzo's finger is now a token of successful murder; but it had been a love token: " 'Tis the first token my father made me send him" (III.iv.34). She presents it to her agent in murder as a tip; with some pride, she assures him it is worth nearly three hundred ducats. Yet she does not intend it as the payment for his services. What began as polite fencing over his recompense quickly turns into a doubly baffling debate that disillusions each of them. Beatrice believes she is being generous in offering "three thousand golden florens;/I have not meanly thought upon thy merit" (III.iv.62–63). He has hinted that his merit is such that he scorns wages; now he is angered as he realizes that she has seen him only as a servant; and her use of "merit," contrasted to his, can be only an insult. De Flores reminds her that money cannot buy a clean conscience. He has told himself that the murder is "but light and cheap/For the sweet recompense . . ." (III.iv.19–20). Nevertheless, though he stresses conscience as overshadowing any fee and thus impresses Beatrice, he cannot escape feeling guilty; for he is stung by conscience several times in the play.

Beatrice has simply not understood what line his hints have taken; she is puzzled, alarmed, fearful: "I'd fain be rid of him. [*Aside*]/I'll double the sum, sir" (III.iv.74–75). Since the offer doubles his displeasure, she urges him to take flight—"And if thou be'st so modest not to name/The sum that will content thee, paper blushes not,/Send thy demand in writing, it shall follow thee . . ." (III.iv.79–81). It is dreadfully ironic for her to use the word "modest." He argues that he will not go without her, that as partners in guilt they belong together, and that she should kiss him "with a zeal"—grant him the intimacy that her seductive behavior in the hiring scene had hinted at. There is additional irony in the term "forgetful" when she warns him that he is forgetting not only his place but also the risk that familiarity will expose them to. He insists that she is being forgetful, reminding her of her indebtedness: "I have eas'd you/Of your trouble, think on it; I am in pain,/And must be eas'd of you . . ." (III.iv.99–100). This statement brings her to half-realization of what her accomplice desires but she attempts to thrust the recognition away, feeling his desire too great an affront to be borne: "I would not hear so much offence again/For such another deed"—upon which, he reminds her that "the last is not yet paid for . . ." (III.iv.106–7).

Then he tells her exactly what he expects. Her horror is such that still she does not fully understand her situation:

> Why, 'tis impossible thou canst be so wicked,
> Or shelter such a cunning cruelty,
> To make his death the murderer of my honour!
> Thy language is so bold and vicious,
> I cannot see which way I can forgive it
> With any modesty. (III.iv.121–26)

" 'Tis impossible . . . I cannot see. . . ." Her lack of realization, her blindness, produces the most cutting irony. For De Flores gives her the wonderful retort: "Push, you forget yourself;/A woman dipp'd in blood, and talk of modesty!" With this repetition of "forget" and "modesty" Middleton achieves a tremendous irony of anticlimax.

Beatrice now regrets the hasty decision that led her to conspire with De Flores, and her feeling is expressed in one of Middleton's most telling metaphors: "O misery of sin! would I had been bound/Perpetually unto my living hate/In that Piracquo, than to hear these words!" She seeks refuge, however, in the conventions of the social system: "Think but upon the distance that creation/Set 'twixt thy blood and mine, and keep thee there" (III.-iv.131–32). Her "there" means away, at a distance, apart; but De Flores finds a new position for "there": "Look but into your conscience, read me there." They are equals in conscience, for she is no more than what murder has made her: "settle you/In what the act has made you; you're no more now . . ./You are the deed's creature . . ." (III.iv.132–37).

His next statement brings home to her the new truth of her condition: "peace and innocency has turn'd you out/And made you one with me." So she has been turned morally out of doors, to be an outlaw, a criminal—for she is basically a wild creature, an outlaw—and one dependent on others' favors; in fact, she is dependent on his favors and his will. He had earlier asserted that he would have his will.

Her "foul villain!" is echoed mockingly by his "fair murderess" (III.iv.141–42). He taunts her with changing her affection—"a kind of whoredom in the heart; and he's chang'd now/To bring thy second on. . . ." Here is more irony; for Alonzo is certainly changed. De Flores issues his ultimatum: unless she surrenders to him, she will never enjoy Alsemero: "I'll confess all; my life I rate at nothing" (III.iv.150). Her reply "De Flores!" is a fine touch revealing her deflation! It prepares for her counterproposal, which she states while kneeling and weeping: all the wealth she possesses. Now she has been stripped of all pretension, she voices her thrilling appeal: "Let me go poor unto my bed with honour,/And I am rich in all things!" De Flores puts her to silence; he values his pleasure above "the wealth of all Valencia." Then comes the ultimate blow that forces surrender: "Can you weep Fate from its determin'd purpose?/So soon may you weep me" (III.iv.162–63).

De Flores had knelt to her earlier, begging her to let him be of service, and now she has knelt to him, imploring mercy. Her fate she sees as vengeance for the murder, and she fears she has been cursed from conception to "engender with a viper first" (III.iv.166). As they leave, De Flores voices their epithalamium: "thou'lt love anon/What thou so fear'st and faint'st to venture on" (III.iv.170–71).[32] This scene, with its magnificent dramatic poetry, some of which T. S. Eliot placed on a par with that of Shakespeare or Sophocles,[33] is the highest point of Middleton's tragic dramas.

Act IV opens with a dumb show (one is reminded again of *The Mayor of Queenborough*) which quickly pantomimes concern over Piracquo's disappearance, Vermandero's choosing of Alsemero as husband for his daughter, and the wedding of Beatrice and Alsemero. As De Flores smiles at the way events have developed, Alonzo's ghost appears to him, showing the hand which lacks one finger. The appearance of the ghost is a reminder to De Flores' conscience and a projection of his secret thoughts; for De Flores cannot get away from the *deed* of murder. When he is greeted as a friend of Alonzo's by Tomazo de Piracquo, he says in an aside: "Methinks I'm now again a-killing on him,/He brings it so fresh to me"; and "His company even overlays my conscience" (IV.ii.45–46, 57). Tomazo ironically thinks him honest and helpful: "He'll bring it out in time, I'm assured on't" (IV.ii.59), but he later feels infected by the presence of De Flores and strikes him. De Flores cannot strike back, being inhibited by his sense of guilt; and he also acknowledges the rightness of Tomazo's subtle instinct. Just before De Flores and Beatrice perpetrate their second murder, the ghost again appears, causing alarm and fear in Beatrice and making De Flores speak of "a mist of conscience" (V.i.60). Middleton thus enforces upon his audience the moral order of the world.

Beatrice is now married to the man she desires; but, confronting her wedding night, she fears that Alsemero may discover the truth about her, because her husband, she says, is "So clear in understanding, . . ./Before whose judgment will my fault appear/Like malefactors' crimes before tribunals . . ." (IV.i.-6–8). She is right to fear; for, as Miss Bradbrook indicates, Alsemero's "will does not overpower his judgment." [34] Finding that Alsemero has a book with a description of a virginity test and suspecting that he will give it to her, she memorizes certain responses to ensure her passing it. But to make doubly sure, she bribes her woman Diaphanta, who passes the test satisfactorily, to take her place in the bridal bed. When Jasperino tells Alsemero that he and Diaphanta have heard Beatrice and De Flores talking intimately, suspicion leads him to give his bride the virginity test, which, of course, Beatrice passes.

Diaphanta has agreed to leave Alsemero's bed by midnight, but pleasure keeps her there. Her unreliability is fatal; Beatrice quickly resolves upon her death, and forty lines later De Flores has independently decided to kill her (V.i.5–7, 45–47). The action thus bears out Beatrice's statement: "Murder, I see, is followed by more sins" (III.iv.164). To carry out his plan, De Flores sets fire to the house. There is some element of spectacle here though not so considerable as in *Mayor*. More important for the theme of the play, Beatrice says: "I'm forc'd to love thee now,/'Cause thou provid'st so carefully for my honour" (V.i.47–48). All during the fire episode, in fact, she is emphasizing her love for the ugly De Flores. The irony of De Flores's remark about Diaphanta, "O poor virginity,/Thou has paid dearly for't" (V.i.103–4) is outdone by Beatrice's brazen insistence that her lover be rewarded for his service.

One must suppose that some time elapses between the wedding

night and the final scene; but the authors hurry straight on to have Jasperino place Alsemero where he can observe that his wife and De Flores have had a meeting. In the source, Alsemero, having inexplicably become intensely jealous, taxes Beatrice with infidelity, whereupon she tells him that De Flores committed murder at her request so she could be married to Alsemero. Alsemero raises no issue regarding the murder. After her confession, Beatrice no longer troubles to conceal her scandalous behavior with De Flores, and her jealous husband surprises them together.

In *The Changeling,* Alsemero thinks that Beatrice's loathing of De Flores only masks her true feeling and that her modesty only masks her sensuality. When he throws in her face her "tender reconcilement" (V.iii.50) with De Flores and accuses her of adultery, she declares that she is no adultress but a "cruel murderess" (V.iii.66). She explains the circumstances and bids him: "Forget not, sir,/It for your sake was done" (V.iii.78–79).

Beatrice remains blind; she does not know her husband. Although Alsemero volunteered to challenge Piracquo, he is not the man to connive at her greater crime even though it was done for his sake.[35] He is appalled at the situation he is in. De Flores corroborates Beatrice's confession and her husband's suspicion of her infidelity. "O cunning devils!" cries Alsemero. "How should blind men know you from fair-fac'd saints?" (V.iii.109–10) But the eyes of the blind are opened, and infamous truths lie visible. When her father calls to her, Beatrice responds:

> O, come not near me, sir, I shall defile you!
> I am that of your blood was taken from you
> For your better health; look no more upon't,
> But cast it to the ground regardlessly,
> Let the common sewer take it from distinction.
> (V.iii.152–56)

Upon De Flores, she says, hung her fate. She realizes now her fatal likeness to him which for so long had made her repel him: "She instinctively feared in him that which was latent in her."[36] She sees herself as that De Flores-evil, that defilement to others which Tomazo has sensed in De Flores as a poison and infection.

The subplot of *The Changeling* involves a January-and-May couple, old Doctor Alibius and his young wife Isabella. He is proprietor of a sanatorium for fools and madmen, where, being very jealous of his wife, he has her locked up during his absences by his man Lollio. She resents this treatment, and one might expect her to retaliate upon her husband by having her "will" and cuckolding him. She is given this opportunity by two men of the household of Vermandero, who wear disguises—Antonio as a fool and Franciscus as a madman—to gain entry to Alibius' establishment to seduce his wife. Besides this pair, Lollio also insists upon having a share of her favors should she slip. But she does not.

Isabella's situation is roughly similar to Beatrice's; the authors of the tragedy evidently desired to parallel the main plot with their subplot.[37] Miss Bradbrook developed the idea that the subplot "acts as a kind of parallel or reflection in a different mode: their relationship is precisely that of masque and antimasque. . . ."[38] "Antimasque" is an appropriate term to use for the grotesque comedy of Rowley's subplot; for, set on a lower social level, it involves characters pretending idiocy and madness yet suffering from the madness of love which induces crime in the main plot. Although Isabella is surrounded by real and pretending madmen, she keeps sane.

The theme of appearance and reality is touched on when she disguises as a madwoman and is not recognized by her would-be lover. Various links of imagery between the two plots have been noted by commentators. The title, too, is meant to link both plots. As Holzknecht has pointed out, there is more than one changeling in the play: Antonio pretends to be a changeling, in the sense of halfwit; Beatrice is also a changeling, in the sense of a fickle person; and Diaphanta is a changeling, in the sense of a person secretly exchanged for another.

The two plots are drawn together in the last two scenes. In the rapid dénouement, the deaths of the guilty pair produce the automatic satisfaction of Tomazo's vengeance. There remain an explicit commentary on the theme of changes—Alsemero's statement (V.iii.199–206) being paralleled by those of Antonio, Franciscus, and Isabella—and, with Alsemero's resolve to be a son to Vermandero, the assurance of a return to the moral order.

In both of Middleton's great tragedies, the blindness of the protagonists is the salient theme. The good characters are blind to evil; the bad characters, blind to good; and all of them stumble into fatal situations. Both Bianca and Beatrice make discoveries about themselves, but their insight amounts to supersophistication; they become hardened and boldened, not softened and abashed; depraved, not penitent.[39] Middleton has no illusions about sin and no help for those who embrace it. He watches their dreadful, inevitable decline and fall with merciless eyes.

# CHAPTER 9

# *Assessments*

ALTHOUGH Middleton made his living as a Jacobean dramatist and is, in fact, regarded today as the complete Jacobean, his successes in the theater probably gave him no more contemporary reputation than would come nowadays to a Hollywood writer of scenarios. His contemporaries mentioned him little,[1] no commendatory verses were written about him when he died, and his works remained uncollected until the nineteenth century. John Cotgrave's *English Treasury of Wit and Language* (1655) includes a considerable number of passages by Middleton;[2] but, by the eighteenth century, his writings had been forgotten. Although Robert Dodsley's *Old Plays* made his name somewhat known after 1744,[3] revival of his reputation came with the nineteenth century, from Charles Lamb's *Specimens of English Dramatic Poets* (1808),[4] the collections of his works edited by Alexander Dyce and A. H. Bullen, and the criticism of Algernon Swinburne and A. W. Ward. Twentieth-century scholarship has supplanted biographical guesswork with accurate information, and it has also placed Middleton's achievement in a much more exact perspective than earlier critics did.

## I *Review of Criticism*

The views of Victorian critics and scholars were influenced by their prudishness, their conviction that literature should serve an obvious didactic purpose, and their feeling that the well-made play of the nineteenth century was superior in structure to most Elizabethan plays. They found the subject matter of many Jacobean dramas gross and disgusting. Even Swinburne—although he praised the city comedies for "the vivid variety of incident and intrigue, the freshness and ease and vigour of the style, the clear straightforward energy and vivacity of the action"; *The Changeling* for its skill in presenting the affinity between Beatrice and De

Flores; and *Women Beware Women* for its eloquence and skill of exposition—thought the underplot of *Women Beware Women* "repulsive beyond redemption by elegance of style" and the dénouement "preposterous beyond extenuation. . . ."[5] Ward also regarded some things in both tragedies as revolting, ghastly, gross, and coarse. Middleton, he said, lacked "both delicacy of feeling and sustained earnestness." Yet Ward also found much to commend: the rapidity of movement of Middleton's plays, the author's "constructive skill" and "absence of effort," his "freedom from bombast" and the fluency of his verse; and, surprisingly enough in spite of his reservations concerning some plays, Middleton's intentness "upon drawing faithful pictures of men and manners such as shall . . . bring home the straightforward lessons of morality and virtue which it is in the power of the comic muse to teach"; for, Ward said, "there is no hollowness about his principles as to the conduct of life. . . ."[6] Courthope (1903), however, was more severe: he said that, "as his [Middleton's] highest aim was to gratify the vulgar curiosity of a somewhat vulgar audience, Middleton's genius never rose into the regions of true art." His work, Courthope thought, has too many improbabilities, and he decided that Middleton's was a "completely cynical view of human nature."[7]

Schelling (1908) found Middleton "the most absolute realist in the Elizabethan drama"; he viewed life as a man of the world sees it "and not as the moralist presents it." He thus contrasted Middleton with Jonson the moralist and caricaturist as one who has a comparatively narrow scope because of his worldliness and "blindness to the romance of life." Middleton's art he considered limited by his virtues of moderation to an "adequate but uninspired realism."[8] Since the 1920's criticism has focused on the following questions: the extent to which Middleton is a realist, a satirist, or a moralist; to what extent he has a determinable "personality"; and according to what principles of art his dramas were constructed and achieved their effects.

Miss Lynch (1926) thought that Middleton was indebted to Jonson for "humours" characters and that he used these types much as Jonson did—but only "to give variety to his dramatic pattern"; for he "never illustrates Jonsonian principles with any evident conviction of their philosophical supremacy." She considered Middleton "the greatest realist in Elizabethan drama," a writer especially interested in the spectacle of Jacobean social unrest and the first to show "the fashionable leisure class" exerting "through its . . . pressure on middle class life, a social authority hitherto unrealized on the comic stage." [9] His work was thus an important link between Jacobean and Restoration drama.

T. S. Eliot (1934), who agreed with Miss Lynch about Middleton's realism and who praised him for greatness in both comedy and tragedy, found him so extremely impersonal that "his greatest tragedies and his greatest comedies are as if written by two different men. . . . He remains merely a name. . . . He has no point of view." [10] Eliot's opinion was held in deference by many, but it satisfied few specialists in the field. More detailed studies soon made it clear that Middleton's work does show a definable "personality" and that a consistency runs through the whole body of his writings.[11]

L. C. Knights (1937) has denied that Middleton was a "great realist" and has maintained that his rendering of the material of London life is merely general and conventionalized. He did grant that Middleton's backgrounds provided "some theatrical verisimilitude for his thoroughly improbable plots," but he rated the comedies of intrigue low as literature. Knights found Middleton's satire deficient, for he thought Middleton had nothing to set against the standards of the citizens he wrote about—"neither an aristocratic code nor a popular tradition." [12] Knights' derogatory views of Middleton have had scant effect. While granting the improbability of plots, Henry W. Wells (1940) declared that Middleton's combination of homely London settings with fantastic plots put him "midway between romantic poetry and the conservative comedy of manners" and allied him with Shakespeare; Middleton's *No Wit, No Help,* for example, resembles Shakespeare's *Twelfth Night* for its combination "of wit and tenderness, realism and romance." [13] Middleton is still being praised as a realist. John D. Jump (1955) called him "more completely and exclusively than any of his contemporaries, a realist." But Jump acknowledged that in his poetic dramas Middleton commanded different resources from those of a modern naturalistic writer.[14]

Middleton's special poetic style has been recognized as extraordinarily effective. Miss Bradbrook (1935) credited Middleton with high achievements through simple means. He could write dialogue "of the greatest ease and naturalness," and his language effects were created through implication, through a "pregnant simplicity" seldom found and difficult to achieve. In the same vein, F. P. Wilson said that "the writer who next to Shakespeare gets the profoundest effects of tragedy with the utmost plainness of speech is Middleton."[15] The understatement of Middleton so impressed T. B. Tomlinson (1964) that he called his dramas naturalistic and classed them with those of Ibsen and Chekhov. But Ribner (1962) is probably nearer the mark in stressing his psychological realism and his use of scenes that "are often ritualistic and symbolic."[16]

From the Victorian suspicion of Middleton as an immoral writer, opinion has veered to regard him as a highly moral one. The mid-twentieth century does not expect poetic justice and does not boggle at the getting off without punishment of the successful intriguer in comedy.[17] As for tragedy, recent critics see Middleton as a clear-eyed, ironic, but not exactly detached dramatist. Wells (1940) stressed his acceptance of the traditional "law that the wages of sin is death." In Ribner's view (1962), Middleton's world is governed by an inexorable force of "divine retribution"; and his plays are "conditioned by a Calvinistic bias." R. B. Parker pointed out that Middleton was pulled between his brilliant comedy of manners based on satiric observation and "a desire to denounce immorality."

In early comedies like *Phoenix* and *Your Five Gallants,* the two elements remain unfused; later the moral element is played down; only rogues remain in the comedies, and they have to "punish each other." Parker applies Bergson's comic theory to Middleton's later comedy: when human behavior becomes mechanical, it arouses laughter, and thus the mechanic neatness of the comic intrigues "automatically reduces the solemnity of the punishments." Nevertheless, Middleton was uneasy in the absence of moral condemnation of evil, his plays have many "outcroppings" of criticism, and he tends to resolve the difficulty with grotesque exaggeration. Parker's is a plausible explanation of Middleton's "polarities: a completely amoral vitalism and a more than Calvinistically determined scheme of retribution."[18]

## II *An Estimate of Middleton*

In the transition from the Medieval scheme of things to the modern, the early Jacobean period was the crux—an age poised with extraordinary tension between old and new. It was felt to be a period of unusually rapid social change in which the middle class was gaining more power at the expense of the landed gentry —and at the expense of the traditional decencies of life. At the same time, old certainties regarding the universe had been put in doubt by the "new Philosophy." Thus it was an age of questioning and, in contrast to the Elizabethan period, of greater sophistication.[19] The mood of the time expressed itself in realism and satire; in great tragedy; and in rich, tense, exciting poetry. Middleton made many typical and some exceptional contributions to the Jacobean literature.[20]

In his different plays, as in those by others of the period, didacticism and irresponsibility, realism and fantasy, comedy and satire are mixed in different proportions. There is more didacticism in *The Phoenix* than in any of Middleton's later comedies. There is more sustained satire in *Your Five Gallants* than in his other city comedies. In them, a comedy of intrigue in the Latin-Italian tradition predominates; but it is still a comedy with much incidental satire, as are the comedies of Shakespeare and of Dekker. Greed and lust, with their objectives of money and pleasure, respectively, are emphasized as perennial motives in this comedy of realistic backgrounds.[21] In the city comedies, one of Middleton's purposes is satirical exposure in particular of lawyers, usurers, and social climbers, and in general of the hypocrisies and pretensions of Jacobean society. In some of his works an older, better age with more humane values is explicitly suggested; and in others such an age is generally implied. The standards of such a time are what Middleton set against the city activities that he exposed. Yet it is true, as Miss Lynch and others assert, that he does not maintain, as Jonson did, a solid, philosophically based position of satire.

In the flexibility and grace of his writing (especially of the poetry of his later comedy), Middleton is most like Fletcher of all his contemporaries. He resembles Fletcher, too, in presenting dilemmas (in tragicomedy); in showing intrigue-enmeshed characters; and, finally, in rendering the struggles of sinful characters without reference to a pattern of cosmic forces.[22] But Middleton's dramas, even the farces, have deeper roots in the actual Jacobean world and in the understanding of forces operating there, and his tragedies and tragicomedies have greater depth than Fletcher's.

The temper of the twentieth century is so much like that of the

Jacobean age that one automatically approves of Jacobean writing. Questioning attitude, skepticism, cynicism, satire, amusement, horrors—all the Jacobean fare is congenial. This age cannot but respond to Middleton, the complete Jacobean, with pleasure and look at the world with almost his same eyes. Long ago his powers of construction and rapidity of dramatic movement were recognized, and Richard Levin's analyses have enabled one to understand better how functional Middleton's organizational principles are. But the twentieth century is especially impressed by his psychological realism; by his natural, believable characters and, in particular, by the vividness with which he represents women of different kinds, ages, and classes; by his astringent, cool manner; and by a style appropriate to the realism, the characters, and the manner.

Thus Middleton's reputation is now higher than it has ever been before. Barker ranks Middleton just below Shakespeare and Jonson as "the third great dramatist of the Jacobean stage";[23] and this view is becoming the accepted one. Though much of Middleton's writing—which comprises a substantial quantity—is only journalism or the merely competent drama of the free-lance professional, several of his plays stand out as excellent among their kinds: among the comedies, there are *A Chaste Maid in Cheapside, A Mad World,* and *A Trick to Catch the Old One*, with *Michaelmas Term, The Old Law,* and *No Wit, No Help Like a Woman's* not far behind; in tragicomedy, *A Fair Quarrel;* and in tragedy, *Women Beware Women* and *The Changeling,* although *The Mayor of Queenborough* also has passages and scenes of great interest and power.

Tomlinson stresses Middleton's control, his clearsightedness, his intelligence.[24] For his intelligence, this era most respects him; his seems more a modern intelligence than that of any other Jacobean writer. Observant, analytical, objective, realistically willing to depict the deepest, lowest, most sordid yet most understandable motives and actions of human beings as they contend with their human condition, Middleton makes all plain, in his plain (yet not too plain) style.

His is really an undecorative, functional style, which, as has earlier been indicated, is capable of a variety of uses. In *The Mayor of Queenborough* and in the other tragedies, the pressure of imagination that produced Middleton's poetry translated thought into untranslatable images. His poetry at its best approaches the Metaphysical style; it is akin to the poetry of John Donne and George Herbert.

For all these reasons Middleton's work smacks less of the study than that of any of his contemporaries except Shakespeare. He has not escaped, and never will escape, as completely into "all time" as Shakespeare did; but he speaks in such tones that one can read him very nearly as one's contemporary.

# *Notes and References*

*Chapter One*

1. Unless otherwise stated, all the factual material on Middleton's life comes from Mark Eccles, " 'Thomas Middleton a Poett,' " *Studies in Philology*, LIV (1957), 516–36.

2. On grammar schools see J. Howard Brown, *Elizabethan Schooldays* (Oxford, 1933), pp. 13–15; Craig R. Thompson, *Schools in Tudor England* (Washington, 1958), pp. 9 ff.

3. Eccles, "Thomas Middleton's Birth and Education," *Review of English Studies*, VII (1931), 431; Mildred G. Christian, "An Autobiographical Note by Thomas Middleton," *Notes and Queries*, CLXXV (October 8, 1938), 259–60.

4. *The Works of Thomas Middleton*, ed. A. H. Bullen (London, 1885–86), VIII, 102, 103, 104. Referred to hereafter as Bullen.

5. Edwin Nungezer, *A Dictionary of Actors* (Ithaca, 1929), p. 244.

6. *Henslowe's Diary*, ed. R. A. Foakes and R. T. Rickert (Cambridge, 1961), pp. 201, 205, 206, 207.

7. F. P. Wilson, ed., *The Plague Pamphlets of Thomas Dekker* (Oxford, 1925), p. 223; F. P. Wilson, *The Plague in Shakespeare's London* (Oxford, 1927), p. 112.

8. Schoenbaum believes that Middleton's role in Part I is "negligible" and that the play should not be included in the Middleton canon. S. Schoenbaum, "Middleton's Share in 'The Honest Whore,' Parts I and II," *Notes and Queries*, CXCVII (January 5, 1952), 3–4.

9. Cf. Samuel Schoenbaum, "A New Middleton Record," *Modern Language Review*, LV (January, 1960), 82–84.

10. J. B. Heath, *Some Account of the Worshipful Company of Grocers of the City of London* (London, 1854), p. 410. R. H. Barker quotes a somewhat longer extract in *Thomas Middleton* (New York, 1958), p. 18.

11. Bullen, I, l–li.

12. J. R. Moore, "The Contemporary Significance of *A Game at Chesse*," *Publications of the Modern Language Association*, L (1935), 761.

13. T. M. Parrott and R. H. Ball, *A Short View of Elizabethan*

*Drama* (New York, 1943), p. 169; Barker, pp. 21–23; *A Game at Chesse,* ed. R. C. Bald (Cambridge, 1929).

14. R. C. Bald, "Middleton's Civic Employments," *Modern Philology,* XXXI 1933), 75–76; Robert Withington, *English Pageantry* (Cambridge, Mass., 1920), I, 234–35.

*Chapter Two*

1. *The Complete Works of Algernon Charles Swinburne,* ed. Sir Edmund Gosse and Thomas James Wise (London, 1926), XI, 403; Bullen, VIII, 297.

2. Detailed analysis of *Wisdom Paraphrased* is in Norman A. Brittin, "The Early Career of Thomas Middleton" (Unpub. Ph.D. Diss.), University of Washington, 1947.

3. J. W. H. Atkins, *English Literary Criticism: the Medieval Phase* (New York, 1943), pp. 26–27, 100; William G. Crane, *Wit and Rhetoric in the Renaissance* (New York, 1937), p. 63; T. W. Baldwin, *William Shakspere's Small Latine and Lesse Greeke* (Urbana, 1944), II, 138, 174.

4. Middleton's non-dramatic works discussed in this chapter, except for *The Ghost of Lucrece,* are in Bullen, Vol. VIII. References will be given in parentheses in the text to page or to page, book, and stanza.

5. The stanza beginning "O you that practise" (145) has, for example, Apostrophe, Asyndeton, Climax, Synathroismus, Anthypophora, and Prozeugma; and cf. the first six stanzas of Ch. VIII.

6. Cf. the six stanzas paraphrasing III: 5–7 (161–62).

7. Note, for example, the paraphrase of I: 7–8, and the series of extended similes in V: 9–13.

8. The borrowings from Greene provide a hint regarding Middleton's methods of composition. Since Middleton skipped about in *Ciceronis Amor* as he selected the material he used, one surmises that he kept a commonplace book in which he wrote excerpts from his reading judged useful for ornamenting and augmenting his own verse. Grammar-school masters encouraged pupils to follow this practice as they composed Latin verses.

9. The poems of *The Mirror for Magistrates* are complaints; Thomas Churchyard's *Shore's Wife* (published in the 1563 edition of the *Mirror*) initiates the series of poems on female honor which comprises Samuel Daniel's *The Complaint of Rosamund* (1592), Thomas Lodge's *The Complaint of Elstred* and A.C.'s (probably Anthony Chute's) *Beawtie Dishonoured written under the title of Shores Wife* (both 1593), and Michael Drayton's *Matilda* (1594). Shakespeare's *The Rape of Lucrece* (1594) and Richard Barnfield's *Legend of Cassandra* (1595) are narratives very similar to complaints in content and style.

10. *The Ghost of Lucrece,* pp. xxxi–xxxii.

11. *Ibid.*, p. xix.

12. Donald Lemen Clark, *Rhetoric and Poetry in the Renaissance* (New York, 1922), pp. 95–96; Barker, pp. 26–27.

13. On social and economic conditions cf. Thomas Wilson, *A Discourse upon Usury,* ed. R. H. Tawney (London, 1925); R. H. Tawney, *Religion and the Rise of Capitalism* (New York, 1926); Kate L. Gregg, *Thomas Dekker: A Study in Economic and Social Backgrounds* (Seattle, 1924); Edwin Maslin Hulme, *A History of the British People* (New York, 1924), Ch. 13.

14. R. M. Alden, *The Rise of Formal Satire in England* (Philadelphia, 1899), pp. 159, 160. Earlier English satirists seem naturally to have enjoyed using realistic incidents and local color: *e.g., London Lickpenny* (*anon.*) and Barclay's *Ship of Fools.* Some of Guilpin's epigrams show London scenes.

15. J. Q. Adams (*The Ghost of Lucrece,* p. xix) took the first step in appreciation of and discrimination among the satires; he commended III, IV, and V, indicating particular pleasure in Superbia's description of the banquet room. But V is less good than III and IV, being too palpable an imitation of Marston, containing more rant, and lacking convincing details.

16. This is the title of the second edition (1604); the first edition (1604), containing two instead of three tales, was entitled *The Ant and the Nightingale: or Father Hubburds Tales.*

17. *The Life and Complete Works of Robert Greene,* ed. A. B. Grosart (The Huth Library, 1881–83), X, 237. For the significance of the title cf. "The Night is the Diuells Blacke booke, wherein he recordeth all our transgressions." Thomas Nashe, "The Terrors of the Night," *Works,* ed. R. B. McKerrow (Oxford, 1958), I, 345.

18. The other two came out in 1606: (1) an anonymous *The Returne of the Knight of the Poste from Hell . . .* ; (2) Dekker's *Newes from Hell: Brought by the Diuells Carrier.*

19. Perhaps Middleton got the idea of the disguises from Lodge's *Wits Miserie,* in which Vainglory "appeareth in divers shapes to men. . . ." Lodge also tells how he walks in Paul's and goes to the Royal Exchange, as does Middleton's Lucifer. (London, 1596), p. 3.

20. Paul Lehmann, *Die Parodie im Mittelalter* (Munich, 1922), pp. 234–35; G. Peignot, *Choix de Testamens anciens et modernes* (Paris, 1829), II, 247 ff.; George Kitchin, *Burlesque and Parody in English* (Edinburgh, 1931), p. 25.

21. *Jyl of Brentfords Testament, by Robert Copland Booke-Prynter, The Wyll of the Deuyll and his Last Testament,* ed. Frederick J. Furnivall (London, 1871), p. 20.

22. George Philip Krapp, *The Rise of English Literary Prose* (New York, 1915), p. 488.

23. Since Middleton and Dekker were closely associated as they worked on their pamphlets, and Dekker's *The Wonderfull Yeare* (1603) also has a mixture of verse and prose, that pamphlet perhaps gave Middleton the idea for such a mixture. Cf. Wilson, *The Plague Pamphlets of Thomas Dekker*, pp. xix–xx.

24. Thomas Wilson, *A Discourse upon Usury*. Intro. by R. H. Tawney (London, 1925). pp. 33–34, R. H. Tawney, *Religion and the Rise of Capitalism* (New York, 1926), p. 140; Barnabe Riche's "Epistle to the Noble Souldiers" in *Riche His Farewell to Militarie Profession* (1581, 1606).

25. It functions like the foreign-visitor device used by Montesquieu, Voltaire, and other eighteenth-century satirists.

26. E. M. Leonard, *The Early History of English Poor Relief* (Cambridge, 1900), pp. 73, 78, 136; C. J. Ribton-Turner, *A History of Vagrants and Vagrancy and Beggars and Begging* (London, 1887), pp. 130–31.

27. The question of whether Thomas Middleton the dramatist wrote the nondramatic works ascribed to him has been best discussed by A. W. Ward, *A History of English Dramatic Literature to the Death of Queen Anne,* rev. ed. (London, 1899), II, 494; C. H. Herford, *Dictionary of National Biography,* XXXVII, 363; H. Dugdale Sykes, "Middleton's Early Non-Dramatic Work," *Notes and Queries,* CXLVIII (June 20, 1925), 435; and J. Q. Adams, ed. *The Ghost of Lucrece.* As Adams states, study "yields abundant evidence, both internal and external, that all five non-dramatic works are the product of the same writer" (p. xvi) and he is the dramatist Thomas Middleton.

## *Chapter Three*

1. Rowland H. Evans, "Realism and Convention in the Action of Middleton's Comedy" (Unpub. Ph.D. Diss.), The Johns Hopkins University, 1942.

2. Mildred G. Christian, "Non-Dramatic Sources for the Rogues in Middleton's Plays" (Unpub. Ph.D. Diss.), University of Chicago, 1932, pp. 52, 89.

3. Barker, pp. 26 ff.

4. Alfred Harbage, *Shakespeare and the Rival Traditions* (New York, 1952), p. 85 *et passim;* Harold Newcomb Hillebrand, *The Child Actors* (New York, 1964; orig. 1926), pp. 268–73.

5. William Power, "Thomas Middleton vs. King James I," *Notes and Queries,* CCII (1957), 534; Baldwin Maxwell, "Middleton's *The Phoenix,*" in *Joseph Quincy Adams Memorial Studies,* ed. James G. McManaway *et al.* (Washington, 1948), pp. 743–53.

6. W. J. Courthope in *A History of English Poetry* (London, 1903),

IV, 228, suggested that Middleton imitated *Measure for Measure* for his plan; but one cannot be certain of this.

7. W. D. Dunkel, *The Dramatic Technique of Thomas Middleton in His Comedies of London Life* (Chicago, 1925), p. 12.

8. Tangle's cure is a variation of that of Crispinus in Jonson's *Poetaster.*

9. Una Ellis-Fermor, *The Jacobean Drama,* ed. 4 (London, 1961), p. 132.

10. References to a play about Samson (I.iii.101–9) suggest late 1602, for Henslowe bought a play with this title (not extant) on July 29, 1602. Yet references to a company of porters (I.iii.109; IV.iii.45–46) point to 1605. Perhaps, as Bald suggested (on other grounds), a play of 1602 was revised about 1606. Bullen, III, 7; *Annals of English Drama 975–1700,* ed. Alfred Harbage, rev. S. Schoenbaum (London, 1964), pp. 82–83; Baldwin Maxwell, "A Note on the Date of Middleton's *The Family of Love* with a Query on the Porters Hall Theatre," in *Elizabethan Studies and Other Essays in Honor of George F. Reynolds* (Boulder, Colo., 1945), pp. 195–200; R. C. Bald, "The Chronology of Thomas Middleton's Plays," *Modern Language Review,* XXXII (1937), 36; Barker, p. 160.

11. "Dekker's Part in *The Familie of Love,*" in *Joseph Quincy Adams Memorial Studies,* p. 726.

12. S. Schoenbaum, *Internal Evidence and Elizabethan Dramatic Authorship* (Evanston, Ill., 1966), pp. 190–91.

13. Richard Levin, *The Multiple Plot in English Renaissance Drama* (Chicago, 1971), pp. 59–66.

14. *The Letters and Epigrams of Sir John Harington,* ed. Norman Egbert McClure (Philadelphia, 1930), p. 301.

15. See Note 13.

16. E. K. Chambers, *The Elizabethan Stage* (Oxford, 1965), III, 440.

17. Alan Gerald Gross, "Middleton's *Your Five Gallants:* The Fifth Act," *Philological Quarterly,* XLIV (January, 1965), 124–29.

18. F. W. Chandler, The Literature of Roguery (Boston, 1907), p. 87; Mildred G. Christian, *Non-Dramatic Sources for the Rogues in Middleton's Plays* (Chicago, 1936); R. C. Bald, "The Sources of Middleton's City Comedies," *Journal of English and Germanic Philology,* XXXIII (1934), 378–79. However, both Margery Fisher ("Notes on the Sources of Some Incidents in Middleton's London Plays," *Review of English Studies,* XV [1939], 283–93) and Barker (pp. 159–60) warn us that because the same incidents appear in more than one pamphlet and possibly Middleton may have heard these anecdotes, we should be cautious about source attribution.

19. Ward, II, 519.

20. Madeleine Doran, *Endeavors of Art* (Madison, 1954), p. 168.
21. Levin, p. 128.

## *Chapter Four*

1. Cf. Bullen, I, xliii.

2. Levin, pp. 182, 193. See also Barker, pp. 76–78; Ellis-Fermor, p. 135; and S. Schoenbaum, "*A Chaste Maid in Cheapside* and Middleton's City Comedy," in *Studies in the English Renaissance Drama: In Memory of Karl Julius Holzknecht,* ed. Josephine W. Bennett *et al.* (New York, 1959), pp. 287–309.

3. Perhaps Miss Buckingham was right in thinking that an epigram in Thomas Campion's *Art of English Poesie* was the source of the Allwit-Whorehound situation. In the epigram, "Barnzy" and "Haruy" parallel Allwit and "the founder"—"So that Barnzy now becomes a cypher,/And himself th'adultrer of Matilda." Elisabeth Lee Buckingham, "Campion's *Art of English Poesie* and Middleton's *Chaste Maid in Cheapside,*" *Publications of the Modern Language Association,* XLIII (1928), 784, 792.

4. Levin, pp. 194–202.

5. Note 2 above, Schoenbaum, pp. 302–3.

6. *Ibid.*, p. 297.

7. In Marston's *Antonio and Mellida,* V.ii, Antonio, allegedly dead, rises from his coffin when Mellida's father wishes he could be restored to life.

8. Note 2 above, Schoenbaum, p. 302.

9. Since it has an unmistakable tinge of Beaumont and Fletcher, it could not have been written before the second decade of the seventeenth century. Barker, p. 181. Schoenbaum now dates it 1612. *Supplement to the Revised Edition, Annals of English Drama,* p. 7.

10. D. J. Gordon, "Middleton's *No Wit, No Help Like a Woman's* and Della Porta's *La Sorella,*" *Review of English Studies,* XVIII (1941), 400–414; Louise George Clubb, *Giambattista Della Porta, Dramatist* (Princeton, New Jersey, 1965), pp. 195–202, 289–93. The *Sorella* material is often called the main plot. Though the play opens with it and it is of a romantic nature, it comprises less than 40 percent of the whole. Barker (p. 181) is right to call it an underplot.

11. Gordon, p. 414.

12. Cf. Clifford Leech, *The John Fletcher Plays* (London, 1962), p. 36.

13. The elements appeared in a "Globe of the world," one side of which was open, and it may be that Zeal's references to fires and flames (Bullen, VII, 226) inspired Sir Gilbert Lambstone's costume as Fire in the device of *No Wit.* Beveril prompts Sir Gilbert in the first words of the speech he should give with "The flame of zeal—";

perhaps another stimulation of the playwright's imagination from the *Magnificent Entertainment.*

14. Middleton was impressed by the image of a sudden storm on a bright day. He used it also in *Trick,* IV.iii.14–16, and *The Mayor of Queenborough,* IV.iii.54–58.

15. Note 2 above, Schoenbaum, p. 308; Barker, pp. 86–87; Clubb, pp. 292–93. Regarding the dénouement of the play, Professor Clubb thinks the revelation of the baby-exchanges "seems contrived," and therefore less effective than the dénouement of *Sorella* (p. 291). She does not give Middleton enough credit, however, for establishing in I.i. Lady Goldenfleece's knowledge of a secret concerning the girls and having "Jane" and Mrs. Low-water discuss the matter in I.ii. Lady Goldenfleece's disclosure of the secret in Act V is justified and not, as Professor Clubb says, brought forth only because "time is running short." Disagreeing with Gordon on this matter, Professor Clubb quotes him as saying that "Middleton cuts the knot most expeditiously." Actually Gordon wrote: "Middleton cuts the knot more expeditiously" (p. 412)—than Della Porta, which is true. Professor Clubb also creates a slightly inaccurate impression by saying that Schelling applied the term "extraordinary excellence" to *No Wit* (p. 292). Schelling wrote: "The Middletonian comedies of London life from *Michaelmas Term* (1604) to *No Wit, No Help Like a Woman's* (in 1613) are of an extraordinary excellence in their kind . . ." (*Elizabethan Drama* [New York, 1959], II, 416).

16. Cf. S. Schoenbaum, "Middleton's Tragicomedies," *Modern Philology,* LIV (1956), 13.

17. Richard Levin draws attention to the following proverbs: No trust is to be given to a woman's word; women have tears of dissimulation as well as sorrow; women naturally deceive, weep, and spin. "Proverbial Phrases in the Titles of Thomas Middleton's Plays," *Southern Folklore Quarterly,* XXXVIII (1964), 144–45.

18. One notices a few links between this comedy and Middleton's other work. When Aurelia's father finds her with Lactantio, Lactantio pretends that she is a foreign gentleman who does not understand the language. The father then speaks some "Latin," accusing her. This resembles the scene with the Dutch merchant's son in *No Wit.* Aurelia's disguise has been betrayed by her servant, an ugly and disreputable-looking fellow of whom she says, "Health cannot be more trusty to man's life/Than he to my necessities in love" (I.i.34–35). The servant reminds one of De Flores in *The Changeling.*

19. Dyce reported that he had a copy of the 1652 quarto in which the names of Jonson and Fletcher were stricken out, and the word *alone,* "written, in an old hand," after Middleton's name. Whatever authority this notation may have, students of the play have not been

able to recognize any evidence of the hands of Jonson or Fletcher. Some have thought Fletcher may have revised the comedy, originally written by Middleton. Cf. Barker, pp. 181–82.

20. H. Dugdale Sykes, *Sidelights on Elizabethan Drama* (London, 1924), pp. 159–72; F. L. Lucas, ed., *The Complete Works of John Webster* (London, 1927), IV, 65–68; Barker, pp. 191–92; W. D. Dunkel, "The Authorship of *Anything for a Quiet Life*," *Publications of the Modern Language Association*, XLIII (1928), 799. Also G. E. Bentley, *The Jacobean and Caroline Stage*, IV, 859–61, who is unconvinced that Webster had anything to do with the play. Metrical evidence makes Barker think Middleton is not the sole author, and Ants Oras has more recently observed that the play "in the parts attributed to Webster by Lucas has almost the pattern [of line-split pauses] of Webster's share in *The Fair Maid of the Inn*. . . ." *Pause Patterns in Elizabethan and Jacobean Drama* (Gainesville, Fla., 1960), pp. 31–32. Since most of the play was printed as prose in the 1662 edition of Kirkman, who first attributed it to Middleton, the blank verse of modern editions is suppositional, and metrical evidence must be heavily discounted.

21. Christian, *Non-Dramatic Sources*, pp. 8, 83, 97.

22. Lucas, II, 215–16, 346–47; IV, 139.

23. Samuel R. Gardiner, *History of England from the Accession of James I to the Outbreak of the Civil War 1603–1642* (London, 1896), IV, 349.

24. Gardiner, V, 129.

25. A detailed account of the negotiations over the Spanish marriage and their aftermath will be found in Gardiner, V, 1–234, and a shorter account in the Introduction to R. C. Bald's edition of *A Game at Chesse*.

26. The *Directions concerning Preachers* forbade preachers to discuss "the Power, Prerogative, and Jurisdiction, Authority, or Duty of Sovereign Princes, . . . or fall into bitter Invectives, and indecent railing Speeches against the Persons of either *Papists* or Puritans." Quoted in Bald's ed. of *Game*.

27. The complete list of pamphlet sources is in Bald's ed. of *Game*, pp. 14–15.

28. *Encyclopaedia Britannica*, 11th ed., VIII, 404; *Catholic Encyclopedia*, V; Bald's ed. of *Game*, pp. 7–10.

29. Moore, p. 764.

30. F. S. Boas, *An Introduction to Stuart Drama* (London, 1946), p. 245.

31. See Bald's ed. of *Game*, pp. 10–13, for the best discussion of the question of character identifications.

32. *Ibid.*, pp. 13, 150–51.

33. The Trinity MS, which Bald used as the basis of his edition, reads: "And there behold the Baggs Mouth, like Hell opens/To take her due . . ." (V.iii.197–98), with the stage direction: "*The Bagge opens, the Bl. Side in it.*" This may indicate that the "bag" part was handled as if the bag were the hell-mouth of the medieval religious drama and that the audience of 1624 was still expected to recognize the medieval stage apparatus. Cf. E. K. Chambers, *The Elizabethan Stage* (Oxford, 1965), II, 528, n. 3.

I believe Bald was right in pointing out (p. 16) that this scene of self-accusation was modeled on the interview of Malcolm and Macduff in *Macbeth,* IV.iii, in which Malcolm, to test Macduff, accuses himself of lust, avarice, and all other vices.

34. Moore, pp. 765, 766.

35. Note, for example, I.i.75–80; 242–66; II.i.56–66; II.ii.17–40; IV.i.46–53; III.i.338–39.

*Chapter Five*

1. As in *The Family of Love* and Dekker and Webster's *Westward Ho!* and *Northward Ho!* gallants are pursuing citizens' wives and are thwarted in their attempts at seduction.

2. George R. Price, "The Shares of Middleton and Dekker in a Collaborated Play," *Papers of the Michigan Academy of Science, Arts, and Letters,* XXX (1944), 607.

3. *Ibid.*, pp. 601–15; Bullen, I, xxxvii; Barker, pp. 170–76.

4. Similar trips to such places are shown in *Westward Ho!* and *Northward Ho!*

5. Another cheating by precontract, as Bullen remarked (I, xxxvii), is in *Trick.* All through the subplot there is much the same material as in Middleton's comedies for Paul's Boys.

6. Canting terms appear in Dekker's pamphlets *The Belman of London* (1608) and *Lanthorne and Candlelight* (1608). Names of such characters as Sir Beauteous Ganymede and Lord Noland are, however, typical of Middleton.

7. Doran, p. 168.

8. Barker, pp. 177–80; C. M. Gayley, *Beaumont the Dramatist* (New York, 1914), p. 378; E. H. C. Oliphant, *The Plays of Beaumont and Fletcher* (New Haven, 1927), pp. 451–57; Dewar M. Robb, "The Canon of William Rowley's Plays," *Modern Language Review,* XLV (April, 1950), 137–38; Cyrus Hoy, "The Shares of Fletcher and His Collaborators in the Beaumont and Fletcher Canon (V)," *Studies in Bibliography,* XIII (1960), 77–92, 104–5.

9. Hoy (p. 92) also suggests the possibility that Middleton and Rowley may have thoroughly revised an original "by Fletcher and one or more unknown dramatists."

10. The fact that Ben Jonson in the Preface to *The Masque of Queens* first used the term antimask in 1609 (though it was probably known to some people a year or two earlier) makes a date of 1609 probable for the play. Herford and Simpson, *Ben Jonson* (Oxford, 1925–52), II, 275–77; X, 500. References in Act V to the New River at Islington, Sir Hugh Middleton's project increasing London's water supply, might easily have been inserted in 1613.

11. For example, all the old men of a tribe are ordered to be killed at a time of famine. One man hides his father. Later when things go wrong in the hands of the young, the old man appears and is able to do certain tasks and to help them with his wisdom. Schoenbaum, "Middleton's Tragicomedies," p. 11 n., with ref. to Stith Thompson, *Motif-Index of Folk-Literature*, V, 227.

12. The date of 1599 for the play is no longer taken seriously. It depended on a literal consideration of III.i.34; "*Born in an.* 1540, and now 'tis 99." These dates were thus given to show the audience clearly that Agatha was 59. Bentley, *Jac. and Car. Stage,* IV, 890. For other matters regarding date see Maxwell, *Studies in Beaumont, Fletcher, and Massinger* (Chapel Hill, N.C., 1939), pp. 138–46; George R. Price, "The Authorship and the Manuscript of *The Old Law,*" *Huntington Library Quarterly,* XVI (1953), 135–39.

13. On authorship see Bullen, I, xv-xvii; Dewar M. Robb, "The Canon of William Rowley's Plays," *Modern Language Review,* XLV (1950), 136–37; Price, above, pp. 117–35; Barker, pp. 184–89; Schoenbaum, Chap. 4, note 16 above, p. 10.

14. Shakespeare, *Troilus and Cressida,* I.iii.107,115.

### *Chapter Six*

1. The story goes back to Paulus Diaconus' *History of the Langobards.* That Middleton used Machiavelli as his source is shown by the name Almachildes (Almachilde in Machiavelli). The *Florentine History* had been translated into English by T[homas] B[edingfield] (1595), but it seems likely that Middleton read the story in Italian. Frank Sullivan, "Thomas Middleton's 'The Witch' " (Unpub. Ph.D. Diss.), Yale University, 1940, pp. 199–200.

2. *The Works of the Famous Nicholas Machiavel* (London, 1680), p. 6.

3. David George asserts that the broken troth-plight of Sebastian and Isabella is imitated from Tourneur's *Atheist's Tragedy.* "The Problem of Middleton's *The Witch* and Its Sources," *Notes and Queries,* XIV (June, 1967), 209–11. The part in which Sebastian tries to gain Isabella's favors by trickery is from Cinthio's *Hecatomithi,* IV, the story of Publio and Iphoromena. Karl Christ, *Quellenstudien zu den Dramen Thomas Middletons* (Borna-Leipzig, 1905),

pp. 25–26; Sullivan, 191–93. Cinthio's next story, as Langbaine noted, was used by Middleton in *A Fair Quarrel.*

4. The witch Medea is quoted in Latin from Ovid's *Metamorphoses,* VII, and then translated (V.ii.18–25). But Middleton might have taken the quotation from Reginald Scot or some other secondary source. Bullen, V, 442, n. 1.

5. Note *Macbeth,* III, v; IV.i.43. Bullen, I, liii-lviii; Henry N. Paul, *The Royal Play of Macbeth* (New York, 1950), pp. 275–76.

6. *The French Academie . . . By Peter de la Primaudaye . . . newly translated into* English by *T. B.* (London, 1586) [orig. French ed., Paris, 1577], p. 314; cf. also pp. 248, 385.

7. [Francis Bacon], *The Charge of Sir Francis Bacon Knight, His Maiesties Attourney generall, touching Duells* (London, 1614), sig. H.

8. Bacon's *Charge,* sigs. G4–G4$^{v}$.

9. Especially Primaudaye, from whom he copied.

10. John Norden, *The Mirror of Honor* (London, 1597), p. 26.

11. It was published in 1617 but may have been produced a year or two earlier.

12. In all the discussion of the play's structure, I am indebted to the illuminating analysis of Richard Levin, *The Multiple Plot in English Renaissance Drama,* pp. 66–75.

13. Barker, pp. 183–84.

14. The idea of making a living by one's wit is the central theme of *Wit at Several Weapons.*

15. *A Proclamation against private Challenges and Combats* (London, 1613).

16. See the excellent discussion by Fredson T. Bowers, "Middleton's *Fair Quarrel* and the Duelling Code."

17. A good man, Primaudaye says, does not measure honor by the opinion of others. "He knoweth (as *Seneca* sayth) that glory is to be followed, not to be desired: that it is gotten by such a noble courage as measureth al things by conscience, not doing any thing for ostentation and vanitie." *The French Academie,* p. 248.

18. There is no doubt of Rowley's verse in II.ii. Note the light endings and indeterminate meter of lines 2, 8, 11, 32, 41, 56, etc. It is doubtful that Middleton could write such a line as "O my hard fate, but my more hard father" (56).

19. Bowers, p. 61.

20. Bowers, pp. 63–64.

21. Levin, *The Multiple Plot in English Renaissance Drama,* pp. 71–74.

22. *Ibid.,* p. 223.

23. H. J. Oliver, *The Problem of John Ford* (Melbourne University Press, 1955), p. 34.

24. Sykes, *Sidelights on Elizabethan Drama* (London, 1924), pp. 183–99; Barker, p. 209; Joan Sargeaunt, *John Ford* (Oxford, 1935), pp. 41–57; Boas, p. 240; E. H. C. Oliphant, *Shakespeare and His Fellow Dramatists* (New York, 1929), II, 18.

25. Kate P. Smith, ed., "The Spanish Gipsy" (Unpub. Ph.D. Diss.), Northwestern University, 1944, pp. lii–liii.

26. However, in *Wisdom Paraphrased* (Bullen, VIII, 170) Middleton contrasts young and old judges, favoring the old.

27. Barker, p. 209.

28. Cf. *Honorable Entertainments,* ed. R. C. Bald.

29. Possibly, as Schelling thought, Rowley may have led the way to this Spanish material, but Schelling's argument that Rowley became interested in Spanish topics through collaboration with Fletcher on *The Maid in the Mill* is spoiled by the fact that *The Spanish Gipsy* was licensed six weeks earlier than *Maid. Elizabethan Drama,* II, 217.

30. Schelling, II, 217–18.

31. Rape of a blindfolded woman had been used in *The Mayor of Queenborough.*

32. K. P. Smith, p. xxxvi.

33. K. P. Smith, p. xcv.

*Chapter Seven*

1. Schelling, *Elizabethan Drama,* II, 97.

2. "The age delighted in the compact expression secured by visual symbolism." "All disadvantages were small before the immense possibilities of symbolism. The age with its allegory and mythology had provided the perfect instrument for bringing to the eye and ear of the monarch the virtues he should ensue and the vices he should avoid." Allan H. Gilbert, *The Symbolic Persons in the Masques of Ben Jonson* (New York, 1965), pp. 14, 26.

3. Withington, *English Pageantry,* II, 3.

4. "Under date of 8 July, 1613, 'it is ordered that the Company of Grocers shall haue two convenient rooms one aboue another beneath in Leaden hall for the workmen to make their pageants and other devises in against the next Lord Maiors day.'" Withington, II, 33, n. 1.

5. Anthony Munday, *Metropolis Coronata, the Triumphs of Ancient Drapery* (London, 1615), sig. A3ʳ.

6. Frederick W. Fairholt, *Lord Mayors' Pageants.* Percy Society, X (London, 1843), pp. 161–69.

7. Jackson I. Cope, "The Date of Middleton's 'Women Beware Women,'" *Modern Language Notes,* LXXVI (April, 1961), 295.

8. In particular, the use of mists of Error and the parting of them

by Truth's fan of stars. Gilbert, pp. 238–43; Herford and Simpson, *Ben Jonson,* VII, 239–40; X, 479, 481.

9. Bullen, VII, 239, n.; Edward Thompson and G. T. Garratt, *Rise and Fulfillment of British Rule in India* (London, 1934), p. 9.

10. Note that Dekker's Envy, however, in *Troia Nova Triumphans* is presented as "a Fury, her haire full of Snakes, her countenance pallid, meagre and leane, her body naked, in her hand a knot of Snakes, crawling and writhen about her arme." *Dramatic Works,* ed. F. Bowers, III, 238. Dekker's Envy was probably based on Ripa's *Iconologia;* Middleton's Envy was apparently created by combining details given in Ripa—the left breast bitten by a snake (cf. Gilbert, p. 88)—and in Alciati's *Emblemata* or in Geoffrey Whitney's *A Choice of Emblemes.* Alciati's Envy (No. 71) is said to be eating her own heart (but is shown eating a serpent and tearing at the heart in her bosom) and is carrying a rude spear in her left hand. Andreae Alciati, *Emblemata* (Ex Officina Plantiniana, Raphelengii, 1608), p. 76.

11. T. S. Willan, *Studies in Elizabethan Foreign Trade* (Manchester, 1959), pp. 93–95; Fairholt, p. 24; Eldred Jones, *Othello's Countrymen* (London, 1965), pp. 145–47.

12. For information on the theme of "Veritas Filia Temporis" see Samuel C. Chew, *The Pilgrimage of Life* (New Haven, 1962), pp. 19–20 and notes. He wrongly says Middleton does not suggest that Truth is Time's daughter.

13. Withington, II, 35.

14. *Ibid.,* II, 37.

15. Middleton probably took the idea of coupling Drake and Jason from Geoffrey Whitney, *A Choice of Emblemes* (1586), Part II, p. 203. Cf. also Rosemary Freeman, *English Emblem Books* (London, 1948), p. 56.

16. Barker, pp. 23–24; also Withington, I, 234–35.

17. W. W. Greg, *A Bibliography of the English Printed Drama to the Restoration* (London, 1962), II, no. 358.

18. Herford and Simpson, *Ben Jonson,* X, 560.

19. On Shrove Tuesday, 1617, the apprentices committed "tumultuous outrages" and did great damage to the *Phoenix* and the property of the Queen's Men. Bentley, I, 161–62.

20. Introduction, Malone Society Reprints, ed. R. C. Bald (Oxford, 1953), p. vi.

21. Samuel C. Chew, *The Crescent and the Rose* (New York, 1965; orig. 1937), pp. 244, 261, 303–5.

22. In *British Museum Catalogue* and STC.

23. Bullen, I, xliv-xlvi; and especially Rhodes Dunlap, "James I,

Bacon, Middleton, and the Making of The Peace-Maker," in *Studies in the English Renaissance Drama: In Memory of Karl Julius Holzknecht,* ed. Josephine W. Bennett *et al.* (New York, 1959), pp. 82–94.

24. Dunlap, p. 85.

25. Dunlap, p. 87. After the king's proclamation against dueling in 1614, his edict was issued, a treatise of 119 pages composed by Northampton. "James . . . had gathered the material he wished to set forth, and had entrusted Northampton to put his thoughts in writing." D. Harris Willson, *King James I and VI,* (New York, 1956), p. 308.

26. Bullen, VIII, 338: "A miserable effect . . . upon the law" is largely from Bacon, pp. 10–11; pp. 338–39: the French example comes from Bacon, p. 18; p. 339: "bewitching sorcery . . . Satanical illusion . . . nations," from Bacon, p. 12; p. 336: the idea about contumely, from Bacon, pp. 19–20.

## *Chapter Eight*

1. See the Note on Works of Doubtful Authorship.

2. Irving Ribner, *The English History Play in the Age of Shakespeare* (Princeton, 1957), pp. 25–26, 267–72.

3. R. C. Bald, ed., *Hengist, King of Kent; or The Mayor of Queenborough,* p. xxxviii.

4. The "rape" has to be by Vortiger, so that he will not be forsworn.

5. R. C. Bald, ed., *Hengist, King of Kent,* p. xlvi; Samuel Schoenbaum, *Middleton's Tragedies* (New York, 1955), pp. 100–01.

6. Bald, Intro. to *Hengist;* Schoenbaum, *Middleton's Tragedies,* pp. 69–101; Barker, pp. 116–21.

7. Barker, p. 119; Schoenbaum, *Middleton's Tragedies,* p. 90.

8. Schoenbaum, *Middleton's Tragedies,* p. 84.

9. *Ibid.,* p. 101.

10. Since *Women Beware Women* was not published until 1657 (*Stationers' Register* entry, September 9, 1653) and no record of a performance is known, its date may fall anywhere between the date of publication of *Des amours tragiques* . . . (Paris, 1610) and a date close to Middleton's death. Its style suggests a later rather than earlier date. J. I. Cope's attempt to date it c. 1614, close to *The Triumphs of Truth* because of references in both to mists of error, is not persuasive. ("The Date of Middleton's 'Women Beware Women,'" *Modern Language Notes,* LXXVI [April, 1961], 295–300.) Opinions divide on whether it was written shortly before *The Changeling* of 1622, or later. On the basis of style Bentley dates it in the last two years of Middleton's life. (*Jac. and Car. Stage,* IV, 907–8.) Ribner places it shortly before his death. (*Jacobean Tragedy*

[New York, 1962], pp. 124–25.) Ornstein, however, is dubious about the late date (*The Moral Vision of Jacobean Tragedy* [Madison, 1960], p. 190.), and Schoenbaum believes 1621 most likely. (*Middleton's Tragedies*, p. 236; *Annals of English Drama 975–1700*, ed. Alfred Harbage, rev. S. Schoenbaum [London, 1964], p. 114.) Although none of the suggested topical references carries certainty, I am impressed by B. Maxwell's suggestion that Middleton changed Duke Francesco's age from 23 to 55 (I.iii.94–96) as a compliment intended for King James because James was 55 in 1621. ("The Date of Middleton's *Women Beware Women*," *Philological Quarterly*, XXII [1943], 338–42.)

11. For the summaries of these stories I am indebted to Professor Schoenbaum, who tells them in much more detail in *Middleton's Tragedies*, pp. 104–14. The information on Bianca's death is in the manuscript of Fynes Moryson's *Itinerary*, published as *Shakespeare's Europe*, ed. Charles Hughes (London, 1903; New York, 1967), pp. 94–95.

12. Cf. Beatrice-Joanna in *Changeling* upon meeting Alsemero.

13. Madeleine Doran (p. 78) reminds us that because of the doctrine of decorum virtuous women in Elizabethan drama "fall simply because they are women and by nature weak."

14. De Flores in *Changeling* feels the same compulsion to be with Beatrice-Joanna.

15. Note the ironic parallel with Livia's action for him in II.i.

16. Revealing the incest, Livia says, "The deed cries shortly in the midwife's arms . . ." (IV.ii.70).

17. Dan S. Norton and Peter Rushton, *A Glossary of Literary Terms* (New York, 1941), p. 81.

18. Ornstein, p. 191.

19. Barker (p. 143): "Drama yields to something like ballet with distinct overtones of symbolism." Ribner (*Jacobean Tragedy*, pp. 151–52) thinks the final scene justified not by the logic of human probability but by theme and passion.

20. For example, when Livia asks Hippolito where he got his "strange affection" for Isabella, he says, "Even as easily/As man comes by destruction, which ofttimes he wears in his own bosom" (II.i.2–4). Leantio remarks that if Florence knew Bianca was in the city, "a pride would take thee/Able to shoot destruction through the bloods/Of all thy youthful sons" (I.i.163–64); and later he speaks of his fear of "a glorious dangerous strumpet,/Sparkling in beauty and destruction too,/Both at a twinkling . . ." (III.i.95–97).

21. Bradbrook, *Themes and Conventions*, p. 224.

22. T. S. Eliot, *Elizabethan Essays* (New York, 1964), p. 94.

23. Schelling, *Elizabethan Drama 1558–1642*, I, 586.

24. Mr. Jump compares it with the verse-instrument that T. S. Eliot desired for *The Cocktail Party*, providing "unbroken transition between the most intense speech and the most relaxed dialogue." Quoted from Eliot's *Poetry and Drama* in "Middleton's Tragedies," p. 355.

25. This reminds one of what De Flores tells Beatrice: "I have eas'd you/Of your trouble, think on it; I am in pain,/And must be eas'd of you . . ." (*Changeling*, III.iv.98–100).

26. Chief materials on the sources of *The Changeling* are Gerard Langbaine, *An Account of the English Dramatick Poets* (Oxford, 1691), p. 371; Bertram Lloyd, "A Minor Source of The Changeling," *Modern Language Review*, XIX (1924), 101–2; E. G. Mathews, "The Murdered Substitute Tale," *Modern Language Quarterly*, VI (1945), 187–95; Martin W. Sampson, ed., *Thomas Middleton* (New York, 1915), p. 402. Others are cited by N. W. Bawcutt, ed., *The Changeling* (London, 1958), pp. xxxi-xxxv. Bawcutt quotes pertinent passages of Reynolds and Digges, pp. 113–29.

27. Bawcutt, p. xxxvii.

28. Bentley, *The Jacobean and Caroline Stage*, IV, 861–64; Bawcutt, pp. xxiv-xxix.

29. Bawcutt conveniently summarizes the evidence on authorship, pp. xxxix-xliii.

30. John Reynolds, *The Triumphs of Gods Revenge against the Crying and Execrable Sinne of (Willful and Premeditated) Murther* (London, 1635), pp. 52, 53.

31. In the course of the play "service," "blood," "will," "act," and "deed" acquire double meanings. Ricks, pp. 291 ff.

32. Cf. "Shrinke not, soft *Virgin*, you will love,/Anon, what you so feare to proue." Ben Jonson, *Hymenaei*, 453–54 (Herford and Simpson, *Ben Jonson*, VII, 225).

33. *Elizabethan Essays*, p. 91.

34. Bradbrook, *Themes and Conventions*, p. 220.

35. *Ibid.*, p. 221.

36. Ornstein, p. 187.

37. This idea is supported by William Empson, *English Pastoral Poetry* (New York, 1938), pp. 48–52 (his ideas on the double plot were expressed in a lecture at Cambridge in 1931); Bradbrook, *Themes and Conventions*, pp. 213–24; Karl L. Holzknecht, "The Dramatic Structure of *The Changeling*," *Renaissance Papers*, ed. Allan H. Gilbert (University of South Carolina, 1954), pp. 77–87; N. W. Bawcutt, ed. *The Changeling*, pp. lxii-lxviii; Ribner, pp. 129, 134–37; Tomlinson, *A Study of Elizabethan and Jacobean Tragedy* (Cambridge, 1964), pp. 200–204; George W. Williams, ed. *The*

*Changeling* (Lincoln, Nebraska, 1966), pp. xviii-xxiv. The older opinion, that the subplot is largely irrelevant, is expressed by Pauline G. Wiggin, *An Inquiry into the Authorship of the Middleton-Rowley Plays* (Radcliffe College Monographs, IX, Boston, 1897), p. 43; Arthur Symons, *Cambridge History of English Literature,* VI, 77; Ellis-Fermor, p. 144; Schoenbaum, *Middleton's Tragedies,* pp. 103, 147; Barker, pp. 129–30.

38. *Themes and Conventions,* p. 221.

39. See the excellent discussion of Edward Engelberg, "Tragic Blindness in *The Changeling* and *Women Beware Women,*" *Modern Language Quarterly,* XXIII (1962), 20–28.

### *Chapter Nine*

1. It is most often remembered that, when Ben Jonson in 1619 was telling Drummond of "his acq̄uaintance & Behaviour with Poets Living with him," he remarked that Middleton, like Day and Markham, "was not of the number of the Faithfull . j . Poets and but a base fellow." *Ben Jonson,* ed. Herford and Simpson, I, 136–37.

2. G. E. Bentley, "John Cotgrave's *English Treasury of Wit and Language* and the Elizabethan Drama," *Studies in Philology,* XL (1943), 197.

3. Dyce, *The Works of Thomas Middleton* (London, 1840), I, 1.

4. But Hazlitt (1820) included Middleton among the majority of Jacobean dramatists "whose names are now little known, and their writings nearly obsolete." "Lectures on the Dramatic Literature of the Age of Shakespeare," in *The Complete Works of William Hazlitt,* ed. P. P. Howe (London, 1931), VI, 193.

5. "Thomas Middleton," in *The Complete Works of Algernon Charles Swinburne,* ed. Sir Edmund Gosse and Thomas James Wise (London, 1926), XI, 391, 400, 406.

6. Ward, *A History of English Dramatic Literature,* II, 514, 538–40.

7. W. J. Courthope, *A History of English Poetry,* IV (London, 1903), 228–30.

8. Schelling, *Elizabethan Drama 1558–1642,* I, 515–17.

9. Kathleen M. Lynch, *The Social Mode of Restoration Comedy* (New York, 1926), pp. 24–26, 28.

10. Eliot, *Elizabethan Essays,* pp. 87, 88, 89, 97. Eliot did not discriminate carefully in plays of double authorship; he praises Middleton for parts of *The Roaring Girl* written by Dekker.

11. Barker, pp. 150–52; Ribner, *Jacobean Tragedy,* pp. 9–10, 123–26, 152; R. B. Parker, "Middleton's Experiments with Comedy

and Judgment," in *Jacobean Theatre* (Stratford-upon-Avon Studies, I) (London, 1960), pp. 179–99; and especially Schoenbaum, "Middleton's Tragicomedies," p. 19.

12. L. C. Knights, *Drama and Society in the Age of Jonson* (London, 1937), pp. 257–61, 266–69.

13. Henry W. Wells, *Elizabethan and Jacobean Playwrights*, ed. 2 (New York, 1940), pp. 223–24, 229; also Barker, p. 63, and Doran, p. 156.

14. Jump, pp. 355–68.

15. Bradbrook, *Themes and Conventions*, pp. 217, 239; F. P. Wilson, *Elizabethan and Jacobean* (Oxford, 1945), p. 107.

16. Tomlinson, pp. 158, 171–72; also Schoenbaum, "Middleton's Tragicomedies," p. 8; Ribner, p. 152.

17. Barker, p. 62.

18. Wells, pp. 38–39; Ribner, pp. 9, 125; R. B. Parker, pp. 179–99.

19. Ellis-Fermor, Ch. 1; Wilson, *Elizabethan and Jacobean.*

20. A. H. Thorndike, *English Comedy* (New York, 1929), p. 166; F. E. Schelling, *English Literature During the Lifetime of Shakespeare.* Rev. ed. (New York, 1927), p. 188.

21. Doran, p. 149.

22. Clifford Leech, *The John Fletcher Plays* (London, 1962), p. 113.

23. Barker, p. 153.

24. Tomlinson, pp. 182–86.

# Selected Bibliography


### PRIMARY SOURCES

1. *Collections*

Two collections of Middleton's works have been issued: (1) *The Works of Thomas Middleton, now first collected, with some account of the Author, and notes*. Ed. Alexander Dyce. 5 vols. London: Edward Lumley, 1840; (2) *The Works of Thomas Middleton*. Ed. A. H. Bullen. 8 vols. London: John C. Nimmo, 1885–86. There is a selection of plays in *The Best Plays of Thomas Middleton*. Ed. Havelock Ellis. With an Introduction by Algernon Charles Swinburne. Mermaid Series, vols. 13–14. London: Vizetelly, 1890. Bullen made little improvement on Dyce's text, and the Mermaid edition is poorly edited. A new text of Middleton's work is a great desideratum.

2. *Separate Works*

Some of Middleton's plays have been well edited in the Revels Plays (Harvard University Press), the Regents Renaissance Drama Series (University of Nebraska Press), and the Fountainwell Drama Texts (University of California Press). Other editions of Middleton's separate works are as follows:

*A Game at Chesse*. Ed. R. C. Bald. London: Cambridge University Press, 1929.

*The Ghost of Lucrece*. Ed. Joseph Quincy Adams. Folger Shakespeare Library Publications. New York: Scribner, 1937.

*Hengist, King of Kent; or the Mayor of Queenborough*. Ed. R. C. Bald. Folger Shakespeare Library Publications. New York: Scribner, 1938.

*Honorable Entertainments*. Ed. R. C. Bald. Malone Society Reprints. Oxford: Malone Society, 1953.

3. *Note on Works of Doubtful Authorship*

Middleton may be the author of some of the works cited below, or of parts of them. At present, evidence of his authorship is not strong enough to warrant their inclusion in the Middleton canon.

*Blurt, Master Constable.* I agree with Price and Barker that this play is by Thomas Dekker. But see David M. Holmes, "Thomas Middleton's *Blurt Master-Constable, or The Spaniard's Night-Walk,*" *Modern Language Review*, 64 (1969), 1–10.

*The True Narration of the Entertainment of his Royall Maiestie, from the time of his departure from Edenbrough; till his receiuing at London. . . .* Printed by Thomas Creede, for Thomas Millington, 1603. Possibly Middleton wrote this pamphlet (bearing the initials T. M.) while the theaters were closed in the spring of 1603.

*The Puritan.* There is a strong likelihood that at least part of this play is by Middleton.

*The Revenger's Tragedy.* Attributed in the mid-seventeenth century to Cyril Tourneur, this play has seemed to several twentieth-century scholars (particularly George R. Price and Peter B. Murray) more likely to be by Middleton.

*The Second Maiden's Tragedy.* Opinion has divided chiefly between Middleton and Tourneur as author though the play has also been attributed to George Chapman.

*The Nice Valor.* This comedy was included in the Beaumont and Fletcher folio of 1647, but internal evidence suggests that Middleton had a hand in the play.

## SECONDARY SOURCES

1. *Bibliography*

TANNENBAUM, SAMUEL A., and DOROTHY R. TANNENBAUM. "Thomas Middleton," *Thomas Middleton (A Concise Bibliography). Elizabethan Bibliographies.* Port Washington, New York: Kennikat Press, 1967; orig. New York, 1940, V.

2. *Material in Books*

BARKER, RICHARD HINDRY. *Thomas Middleton.* New York: Columbia University Press, 1958. Mainly written about 1943, the only other book-length study of Middleton's entire work. Very helpful bibliographies. Rather cursory treatments of works. Tries to demonstrate Middleton's authorship of *Revenger's Tragedy* and *Second Maiden's Tragedy.*

BOAS, F. S. *An Introduction to Stuart Drama.* London: Oxford University Press, 1946. Informative commentary from a conservative point of view; stresses Middleton's interest in sexual passion.

BRADBROOK, MURIEL C. *The Growth and Structure of Elizabethan Comedy.* London: Chatto & Windus, 1955. Provides comparisons of Middleton with his contemporaries.

———. *Themes and Conventions of Elizabethan Tragedy.* Edition 2.

Cambridge: At the University Press, 1952. Helpful on construction and imagery of the two chief tragedies.

DORAN, MADELEINE. *Endeavors of Art: A Study of Form in Elizabethan Drama.* Madison: The University of Wisconsin Press, 1954. Historical criticism useful in placing Middleton in relation to the drama of his period.

ELLIS-FERMOR, UNA. *The Jacobean Drama.* Edition 4. London: Methuen and Company, 1961. Good bibliography. Commentaries on the most important plays with enthusiastic appreciation of Middleton's range of imagination and sympathy.

HOLMES, DAVID M. *The Art of Thomas Middleton: A Critical Study.* Oxford: Clarendon Press, 1970. Published too recently to be used for this study, the book treats the bulk of Middleton's writing.

JUMP, JOHN D. "Middleton's Tragedies," *The Age of Shakespeare,* ed. Boris Ford. The Pelican Guide to English Literature, 2. Baltimore: Penguin Books, 1964. Good analysis of the two chief tragedies, with emphasis on the special quality of the verse.

LEVIN, RICHARD. *The Multiple Plot in English Renaissance Drama.* Chicago and London: University of Chicago Press, 1971. Includes a series of brilliant analyses of Middleton's multiple-plot plays that appeared in journals during the 1960's.

ORNSTEIN, ROBERT. *The Moral Vision of Jacobean Tragedy.* Madison: The University of Wisconsin Press, 1960. Finds in Middleton a cold pitilessness, an indifference to the ideal in human nature, and integrity.

PARROTT, THOMAS MARC, and ROBERT HAMILTON BALL. *A Short View of Elizabethan Drama.* New York: Scribner, 1943. Commentaries interpreting Middleton as a man of his period.

RIBNER, IRVING. *Jacobean Tragedy.* New York: Barnes and Noble, 1962. Sees Middleton as highly moral, and his tragedy as dominated by a Calvinistic strain.

SCHOENBAUM, SAMUEL. *Middleton's Tragedies.* New York: Columbia University Press, 1954. Argues for radical views on Middleton canon (modified later). Good on *Hengist* and *Women Beware Women.*

TOMLINSON, T. B. *A Study of Elizabethan and Jacobean Tragedy.* Cambridge: At the University Press, 1964. Upholds Middleton's "poetic naturalism" and "intelligent" drama against Webster and Ford.

3. *Material in Periodicals*

BALD, R. C. "The Chronology of Middleton's Plays," *Modern Language Review,* XXXII (1937), 33–43. Most thoroughgoing attempt to deal with the topic.

———. "Middleton's Civic Employments," *Modern Philology,* XXXI (1933), 65–78. Gives biographical information and explains traditions and limitations of London pageantry.

———. "The Sources of Middleton's City Comedies," *Journal of English and Germanic Philology,* XXXIII (1934), 373–87. Chief contribution on the topic.

Bowers, Fredson T. "Middleton's *Fair Quarrel* and the Duelling Code," *Journal of English and Germanic Philology,* XXXVI (1937), 40–65. Enlightening analysis in terms of Jacobean concepts of honor.

Bullock, H. B. "Thomas Middleton and the Fashion in Playmaking," *Publications of the Modern Language Association,* XLII (1927), 766–76. Gives Middleton credit for dramatic skill; but because he followed the taste of the day and was too scientific in realism, he was no artist.

Eccles, Mark. "Thomas Middleton's Birth and Education," *Review of English Studies,* VII (1931), 431–41.

———. " 'Thomas Middleton a Poett,' " *Studies in Philology,* LIV (1957), 516–36. Eccles' two articles are the nearest approach to a biography of Middleton.

Moore, J. R. "The Contemporary Significance of *A Game at Chesse,*" *Publications of the Modern Language Association,* L (1935), 761–68. Informative in relation to the times.

Phialas, P. G. "Middleton's Early Contact with the Law," *Studies in Philology,* LII (1955), 186–94. Middleton obtained knowledge of law from family litigation and not from Inns of Court.

Ricks, Christopher. "The Moral and Poetic Structure of *The Changeling,*" *Essays in Criticism,* X (1960), 290–306. Interpretation of character and plot through verbal patterns.

Schoenbaum, S. "Middleton's Tragicomedies," *Modern Philology,* LIV (1956), 7–19. Treats the tragicomedies as transitional in Middleton's development from comedy to tragedy.

# *Index*